Library of
Davidson College

Law and the Search for Community

University of Pennsylvania Press
Law in Social Context Series
Keith Hawkins and John M. Thomas, Series Editors

A complete listing of the books in this series appears at the back of this volume.

Law and the Search for Community

Joel F. Handler

UNIVERSITY OF PENNSYLVANIA PRESS   Philadelphia

Copyright © 1990 by the University of Pennsylvania Press
All rights reserved
Printed in the United States of America

Library of Congress Cataloging-in-Publication Data

Handler, Joel F.
   Law and the search for community / Joel F. Handler.
     p. cm. — (Law in social context series)
   Includes bibliographical references.
   ISBN 0-8122-8201-9
   1. Sociological jurisprudence.   2. Law —United States.
3. Welfare state.   I. Title.   II. Series.
K370.H36 1990
340'.115—dc20   89-29877
                                                                                          CIP

To **Betsy** and our family: **Adam, Ann, Frances, Joanne, Kate, Rachel,** and **Stephen**

Contents

Acknowledgments ix

1. Introduction 1
2. Dependent People: Rights and Due Process 13
3. Regulation and Organization 39
4. Trends in Jurisprudence 62
5. Modern/Postmodern Communitarian Ethics 83
6. Four Examples in the Modern State 107
7. The Material and Social Conditions of Community 143

References 163
Index 173

Acknowledgments

This book builds on much of my previous work. Many people helped me in those projects and I would like to express my appreciation. I thank two very capable research assistants: David Becket and Barbara Siegemund-Broka. They are remarkable young people.

Two of my empirical examples are based on the special education program of the Madison, Wisconsin, School District and eight social service agencies in Los Angeles providing community-based care for the frail, elderly poor. Many parents, teachers, school psychologists, parent advocates, parents, social workers, supervisors, and clients gave generously of their time and encouraged me in my work. I thank them all.

My thanks to several of my colleagues who read parts or all of the manuscript: Drucilla Cornell, Yeheskel Hasenfeld, Keith Hawkins, Lawrence Kupers, Carrie Menkel-Meadow, Frances Olsen, Joel Rogers, William Simon, and Lucie White. I especially want to thank Annette Baier and Richard Bernstein, who encouraged me in the interpretation and application of their work. I also appreciate the editorial help I received from Ruth Veleta at the University of Pennsylvania Press and Mindy Brown.

Thanks to UCLA for providing research support and especially the Law School community for a stimulating and supportive intellectual atmosphere. It's a pleasure to work there.

Chapter 1
Introduction

It is hard to know exactly why old problems come back. One old problem presses upon us with increasing urgency: the precise problem—the subject of this book—is that of dependent people dealing with social welfare bureaucracies. But this is part of larger pressing problems—citizen-agency relationships in the modern social welfare state and the critique of the regulatory state itself. The critique of the regulatory state, in turn, is a reflection of more fundamental issues concerning the individual and the state. It is by now banal to talk of *crises*—of the state, of legitimacy, of liberalism, of law, of modernity itself. As the state has taken on new responsibilities and burdens, as it has spread to all the corners of society and penetrated the intimate relationships between individuals, and the struggle for a decent life, the old questions of autonomy and the tension between people as individuals and as social beings—perhaps the greatest dialectic in modern political thought—have re-emerged with a new urgency. With ordinary people now so bound up with government (and other large bureaucracies), what kind of society are we creating? How can the ordinary person maintain some sense of self in the modern state? How can the government be regulatory and caring in these large, complex, and dense undertakings? How can there be autonomy, dignity, and community in the massive modern state?

About twenty-five years ago, we thought we had answers to some of these questions. Emerging from the post–World War II Eisenhower years of normalcy, a new sense of social justice swept the American political consciousness. Spearheaded by the concern for civil rights for blacks, the state responded to a wide variety of calls for social justice centering on the poor, the aged, the sick, the handicapped, women, consumers, and environmental harms. There was an outpouring of substantive entitlements and social benefits. The social welfare regulatory state spread throughout society.

But how were people to be protected in this expansive state? How were they to be sure that they would receive what they were entitled to? How were they to make sure that government would obey the law and would treat them with justice, dignity, and respect? At the same time that the substantive reach of the state was expanded, so, too, were the procedural due-process protections of the citizen. In a wide variety of relationships with government, citizens were given the right to invoke the rule of law if they felt that the government was acting illegally. Citizens could challenge government action in administrative and judicial proceedings. The extent of the spread of these two phenomena—substantive regulatory law and procedural due process rights—was truly remarkable. In about a decade and a half, the United States experienced a legal rights revolution.

This was the *liberal legal* answer to the re-emergence of the problem of the relationship of the citizen to the expanded modern regulatory state. To protect autonomy, to maintain freedom, and to insure legality in the liberal state, the individual was given the legal armament that historically, in the common law tradition, always was used to protect the individual from the illegality of the state.

As explained more fully in Chapters 2 and 3, these answers seemed to have failed, and it is this failure, I believe, that has given rise to the renewed concerns. I say "seemed to have failed." There is widespread criticism of the *substantive* program of the modern welfare state; for example, that economic and environmental regulation is inept, counterproductive, and is lowering our standard of living without creating corresponding benefits; that despite enormous amounts of money poured into social welfare programs, too many of our citizens are less educated, poorer, and sicker. No longer the "night watchman" of liberal society, but now the incompetent manager of the welfare state, government is now blameworthy; hence, the "legitimation crisis."

While the substantive critique of the modern state is a matter of great dispute, it will not be a central focus of this book. Rather, our concern is with the process side of liberal legalism—the attempt to protect the citizen in her dealings with government. In an important sense, both aspects are inseparable. If there were less regulation, if government were less important in the lives of the citizen, then the citizen would be in less need of legal protections. But the withdrawal of government is not likely to happen, at least on any significant scale, now or in the future. Regulation may take different forms—indeed, that is one of the arguments of this book—but in modern society most citizens, and certainly the ones with whom I am concerned, dependent people, will deal with large government agencies or private agencies operating public programs.

In contrast to the critique of the substantive program of the modern state, there seems little doubt, at least in my mind, as to the general failure of liberal legal due process protections. Formal legal protections do not address underlying maldistributions of wealth and power; and the powerless, in large measure, are unable to use legal protections. Procedural due process protections are not proactive; they require the complaining client. For a variety of reasons, there are many barriers to invoking the system and then achieving substantive results. Many citizens are unable to use the remedy, and this is especially true for the poor, minorities, women, and other dependent people. This story will be told in some detail in Chapter 2.

Thus, in the minds of many critics, the modern social welfare state is doubly faulted. Under the progressive impulse of mitigating the harshness of the market economy, the state has expanded its substantive regulatory reach. No longer can the individual make her way autonomously, relatively free of public restraint. Now, whether in business, employed, or dependent, the individual is enmeshed in the state; she moves slowly, haltingly, or often not at all in a thicket of rules. The problems of the citizen and the regulatory state are compounded by discretion. Despite the masses of legislation, rules, regulations, and administrative orders, most large, complex administrative systems are shot through with discretion, from the top policymakers down to the line staff—the inspectors, social workers, intake officers, police, teachers, health personnel, even the clerks. How they interpret the rules, how they listen to the explanations, how they help the citizen or remain indifferent all affect the substance and quality of the encounter, an encounter made increasingly important because of our widespread dependence on the modern state.

It is this image of frustration, anger, helplessness, and apathy that raises anew questions of individual autonomy and the social bond. Complex, dense, extensive interdependence is no longer a choice; it is a problem. A rich and growing literature addresses interdependence at a number of levels: the ethics and practices of the most basic relationships (parent-child; husband-wife; friends and strangers); poor people and welfare offices; parents and students and schools; business managers and environmental or health and safety regulators; as well as citizen participation in government.

The relationship of dependent people and large-scale public agencies cuts across several of these fields. In three strands of thought in particular—law, the sociology of organizations, and critical theory—I see common descriptive and normative themes: the attack on formalism, liberal legalism, and positivism, and the search for autonomy, community, and decisions based on practical knowledge. There is the rejection of relationships purporting to be governed by hierarchically imposed rules. There is the search for people participating in discretionary decision-making.

In law, there is the realization of the limits of the legal rights revolution in protecting dependent people, consumers, and the victims of discrimination, occupational hazards, and environmental harm. Questions are being raised about command-and-control regulation; there is interest in flexibility, bargaining, and negotiation as regulatory strategies instead of rules and adversary procedures, and the use of law and procedure to *structure*, rather than to *decide*, substantive issues in those areas considered beyond regulation.

The sociology of organizations has taken a similar path although, as far as I can tell, it has not self-consciously established the connection between its theoretical transformation and critical theory. The change here has been the evolution from formal rationalism to the loosely coupled or political-economy models of organizations. Organizations are now viewed as arenas of shifting alliances, subject to the vagaries of the environment; goals, authority, and implementation are contingent. The legal system, of course, operates through organizations; it affects organizations, and is affected by them. The contemporary theories of complex organizations track the contemporary assessment of the efficacy of legal formalism. One of the aims of this book is to draw the connections between the developments in the sociology of complex organizations and parallel thinking about legal systems.

Thus far, organizational sociology has been descriptive. While law reflects values more explicitly than sociological theory does, both have interesting connections to critical theory. The modern/postmodern search for the dialogical community rejects classic liberalism, the promise of governing human relationships through formalism, as well as the epistemological aggrandizement of positivism. Instead, it seeks to break down hierarchy, to explicitly introduce values, commitments, and intuitions into the discourse of action and to create the conditions whereby people talk to each other. In law and contemporary sociological theory, the location of the dialogical community would be in the areas of discretion. It asks: In these spaces, what are the material and social conditions necessary for community?

Most of the literature dealing with community assumes, at least implicitly, voluntary associations of people of relatively equal status—for example, religious, fraternal, spatial organizations, clubs, unions, social movement groups, and so forth. Issues of power and hierarchy among members are rarely discussed. The central question is the tension between autonomy and communal interests. But the relationship between dependent people and social welfare bureaucracies is clearly not equal; it is voluntary in only a tenuous, legal, formal sense. Poor people come to agencies because they need help and have nowhere else to go. Is it possible, then, to have a dialogical community in a relationship that is, at least initially, characterized by great disparities in power, strongly hierarchical, and, for all practical purposes, coercive? I argue that it is possible, and that one can detect the search for the dialogic community in these diverse fields of inquiry.

As distinguished from most of the community literature, which assumes a rough equality of resources and then worries about autonomy in community, with dependent people there is a prior question: How can these people be sufficiently empowered to be able to participate? They first have to become autonomous. This is the issue of power. Once dependent people are able to participate, the issue becomes the *quality of participation*, which is the central issue in the communitarian literature.

The inadequacies of the liberal legal rights regime have been recognized in a broad array of theoretical fields that are seeking new ways of structuring the relationship between the citizen and the state. In various forms and from diverse points of view, the overarching theme is a search for cooperative or communitarian rather than adversarial relations. The fields are: regulation (both social welfare and economic); the sociology of organizations and implementation analysis (including social work practice theory); jurisprudence (critical legal studies, feminist jurisprudence, Continental reflexive law); and modern/postmodern ethics. The three fields—law, the sociology of organizations, and critical theory—have mounted a major attack on formalism. By formalism, I mean the governing of relationships through rules. There are both descriptive and normative agendas in the attack, although the normative elements are more specifically addressed in law and critical theory. Yet, the case is uneasy, because there are values in formalism that are not easily replaced in the alternative visions.

Plan of the Book

Chapter 2, "Dependent People: Rights and Due Process," discusses the development of the legal rights revolution from the mid-1950s, its theoretical and practical goals, where it succeeded, and where it failed. The chapter will point out the limits of substantive entitlements and procedural due process; in programs susceptible to regulation by rules, the rules are enforced *against* the clients or the clients are incapable of exercising procedural rights. The main emphasis, however, will be on programs that *require* discretionary determinations—the programs that we are now focusing on to help the poor get into the mainstream—education, training, employment, economic development, health and mental health. The chapter will review the literature on the programs (why the programs have worked so poorly), emphasize their individualized, discretionary features, the disadvantages that dependent people face in these relationships, and the circumstances under which the legal rights regime fails to protect client interests. Particular attention is paid to the various manifestations of power in the client/bureaucracy relationship.

Chapter 3, "Regulation and Organization," will bring together two fields of knowledge that should, but rarely do, connect. There is a growing literature in the law that questions the efficacy of command-and-control regulation and argues for more cooperative styles. These ideas are coming from a number of different directions: economic regulation (including occupational safety and health); environmental protection; family law (divorce, property, custody); and the litigation explosion (alternative dispute resolution, informal justice, cooperative-style bargaining). The sociology of organizations and implementation analysis provide a theoretical framework for this literature. The social sciences emphasize the complexity and loose coupling of organizations, their internal politics, the influence of external pressures, the role of power and technology, and, generally, the ubiquitousness of discretion throughout systems. Social work practice theory shows how this discretion is applied by front-line officials, the intersection between organizational and client interests. It drives home, in an empirical and theoretical manner, the conclusions of Chapter 2, as to why the dependent person is so disadvantaged in relations with large-scale bureaucracies.

Having made a strong case against the legal rights regime, the chapter introduces a counter-theme—the concerns about cooperative-style regulation. Since underlying power relationships are not addressed, there are problems of failing to achieve regulatory goals and dangers to dependent people. These themes are picked up in subsequent chapters.

In Chapter 4, "Trends in Jurisprudence," three bodies of jurisprudential theory address the problem of legal rules, discretion, and community in the modern state: critical legal studies, feminist jurisprudence, and Continental critical and reflexive law. Critical legal studies and feminist jurisprudence are quite diverse, but certain important strands of these two theories focus on the dysfunctional aspects of the rights regime in terms of human relationships (separation of subject and object, domination, discrimination) and argue for structures that will enhance rather than separate communitarian relationships. Continental law theorists (Habermas, Luhmann,

Teubner) argue that the modern welfare state has unduly legalized important social relationships, creating serious problems for the integration of social systems and human relations. They, too, argue for structures that will facilitate discretionary rather than legalistic decisions.

In Chapter 5, "Modern/Postmodern Communitarian Ethics," the theoretical analysis moves into yet another field of knowledge—contemporary ethical philosophy—which has also been concerned about the need for community in the modern social welfare state. The chapter will set out the communitarian vision of philosophers such as Baier, Bernstein, Gadamer, Habermas, Arendt, Rorty, Rawls, and Sandel. Of particular importance will be the problem of dependent people in such communities, an issue usually ignored by communitarian philosophers. This will require a close examination of the issue of power and the role of trust.

Chapter 6, "Four Examples in the Modern State," will sum up the major strands from the theoretical and practical arguments for community, and then analyze them in the context of informed consent in medicine; special education; community-based care for the frail, elderly poor; and water pollution control in England. In each of these empirical examples, there are two styles of regulation. The major, or dominant style, called *legal-bureaucratic*, is traditional, hierarchical, legalistic, and adversarial. It is the style that forms the basis of the critique of the modern social welfare state. In each of the examples, however, there is a discretionary, cooperative, and perhaps communitarian style, which I call the *participatory exception*. The participatory exceptions will be closely examined in light of the theoretical discussions. In what sense are these examples communitarian (what do we mean by "community" in real-life terms?) and how are the issues of power and participation—the concerns of dependent people—handled? What happens to regulatory goals?

Based on both the theoretical and empirical discussion, Chapter 7, "The Material and Social Conditions of Community," develops a theory of discretionary decision-making and community in the modern welfare state. It discusses the role of professional ideologies, technology, structures and incentives, decentralization, and client empowerment. Good intentions (ideology, goodwill, altruism) are crucial, but not sufficient. Bridging the gap between the ethical philosophers and the social science organizational theorists, I argue that *reciprocal concrete incentives* have to be created so that genuine client participation becomes pragmatically necessary to bureaucratic tasks; in addition, clients have to be given the resources so that they can participate. Both of these points are illustrated in the successful participatory examples in Chapter 6. Programs have to be decentralized and structured to facilitate field-level discretionary decisions. The objection that this will result in the failure of regulatory goals is discussed. Both assumptions are questioned—that strict regulation accomplishes regulatory goals and that cooperative decision-making does not.

The concluding section of Chapter 7 deals with the application of the analysis. In the participatory exceptions, dependent people exercise some measure of empowerment in their relationships with government agencies. They become equal moral agents; their conception of self, of others, and their relationship is changed. I argue that these communities are thus both transformative and constitutive. However, these communities are also partial and transitory. They require special conditions and cannot be applied wholesale throughout the regulatory state. There is still a need and a place for legal rights protections in many areas of social life, but ways also have to be found to encourage the growth of communitarian decision-making in a state increasingly characterized by bureaucratic discretionary relations.

The Place of the Book

I examine the possibility of community at one of the basic levels of the modern state: a single citizen interacting with the line staff of a public agency. The focus thus differs from most of the literature dealing with community and participation, where the emphasis is usually on groups (neighborhood, cooperatives, political) or, more abstractly, on the redesign of democratic political institutions. Most ethical philosophy either is non-specific or vaguely descriptive of social groups or discusses one-on-one relationships in non-public settings (e.g., friends, spouses, children, strangers).

The setting that I examine has its own justification. For reasons stated in the opening paragraphs, citizen-state relations are continuing to take on increasing importance with the spread of the welfare state. We are not talking about minor occurrences, especially when one contemplates the growth and complexity of health care, welfare programs, education, employment programs, and so forth. It would be justification enough if some progress could be made in making these relationships more humane, responsive, and just. In the concluding chapter, I carefully specify the limitations of my analysis and solutions.

While I argue that my approach has importance beyond my examples, it would appear to be inapplicable in many other situations involving dependent people and public agencies. Too often, on an abstract level, we propose universal solutions. I try to specify concrete situations in which fragile communities might develop. I do not think that genuine conversations are feasible with hostile, implacable bureaucracies; there, conflict strategies are necessary to protect dependent people—for example, direct action, legal rights, social movement mobilization. I lay great stress on professional norms and reciprocal incentives; without these, I think that normal bureaucratic pathologies will corrupt conversation.

At the same time, these micro-level examples are connected to the broader literature. I try to show that it may be possible to have a genuine dialogue in what looks like a highly improbable situation. In order to demonstrate my argument, my examples are informed by this wider literature—from the social sciences, policy analysis, jurisprudence, feminist theory, and ethical philosophy. It is from this literature that one can explore the possibilities of structural decentralization to allow the necessary space for conversations to take place, that one can analyze the conditions that will enable willing participants to engage in conversation and determine what kind of conversation is taking place.

At the same time—and in the spirit of dialogue—I think that the analysis here informs the wider literature. At one level, I try to demonstrate the possibilities of dialogical relationships for many people, both dependent clients and line staff, in a significant number of settings. In other words, there are practical, real-life possibilities for the kinds of things that communitarian feminists, dialogical philosophers, and critical theorists are arguing. I also show, though, there are structural conditions necessary for these kinds of relationships. Too often this literature pays insufficient attention to underlying issues of power and incentives. Too often it assumes that removing the barriers to communication will result in the kind of communication envisaged. But power and influence operate in subtle ways; relationships are dynamic, and structural conditions have to be constantly renewed.

In other words, it is not sufficient to give the powerless the opportunity to participate. They will still not be empowered. They also have to be given the incentives and the means. Otherwise, communitarian proposals will suffer exactly the same kind of fate as the liberal legal due process solutions—they will be undermined by the underlying maldistributions of power. This is not speculation. The War on Poverty era ushered in numerous citizen groups in many public programs; for the most part, they became co-opted, serving either to legitimate the organization or as part of the delivery mechanisms. Rarely did they fulfill a democratic role. The same analysis can be applied to democratic participation; the oppressed vote when it is meaningful.

No claim is made here to reform the economic and social structure of the United States. What I do argue, though, is two things: the theoretical importance of the distribution question; and, at least in these kinds of examples, the possibility of restructuring programs and conditions so that clients have the resources necessary to participate. The focus on structure brings in the literature on the sociology of organizations as well as social movement groups. It shows the importance of decentralization and environmental influences on organizations. It also incorporates the importance of groups into the design of programs.

I also argue in Chapter 6 that structural reform is important for communitarian theory. At least in the situations that I examine, I argue that the dichotomy between instrumentalism and the more humanitarian ethical values of communitarian feminism and the dialogical philosophers is false and that instrumental elements in my examples contribute to the ideological and moral redefinition of the participants. Cooperative practices can be instrumental only, but they can also be much more.

In this book, I try to bring to bear a wide range of social science, policy, and philosophical literature to explore micro settings of dependent people trying to get by in their daily lives; at the same time, these examples illuminate the conversations of scholars and philosophers.

A Note on Methodology

One of my purposes is to show widespread and cross-cutting ideas in many fields concerned with citizen-state relations. One method of organizing this material would be to take specific aspects of these relations or subject matters—for example, economic regulation, education, welfare—and see what the various literatures have to say. Another approach would be to organize the material according to academic disciplines. I have chosen instead to organize the analysis in terms of methodologies. Chapters 2, 3, and 4 are arranged in ascending levels of abstraction. Chapter 2 deals with legal and social science policy analysis; Chapter 3 with jurisprudential philosophy; and Chapter 4 with ethical philosophy. I take this approach because I think it important to demonstrate how common concerns are being addressed in the literature. I think that this point is more forcefully made in terms of methodology and abstraction. At the same time, I also want to draw vertical connections between the levels—both in regard to academic disciplines and subject matter. Therefore, in each of the chapters, there are sections that relate the materials to the discussion in the previous chapter. In addition, in Chapter 6, which deals with the specific examples, and in Chapter 7, on the material and social conditions for dialogism, a conscious effort is made to bring back the discussions in Chapters 2 through 5. This involves some repetition, but the presentation is complicated, and I hope that this makes the argument more accessible.

Chapter 2
Dependent People: Rights and Due Process

Arising out of the civil rights movement, a broad concern developed for the legal rights of unrepresented people, including poor, handicapped, mentally ill, or sick people and children and women, among others. Charles Reich, in an important article titled "The New Property," argued that with the growth of the modern welfare state, large portions of the population were now dependent on government for their livelihoods. Reich did not restrict his analysis to social welfare relationships. He included occupational licensing, franchising, employment, and business contracts. For the most part, people were not protected in these relationships which were considered "privileges"; status could be altered by government with few limitations. What was needed, argued Reich, was a new conception of property; these relationships were a new, modern form of property that had to serve the function of old property, namely, protecting individuals in their dealings with government (Reich 1964).

The prime evil of modern relationships with government, according to Reich, is that important individual interests are subject to arbitrary, discretionary decisions by government without the restraints or protections of law. Under traditional property relationships, government is constrained in one of two ways. Either the citizen has a clear, legal entitlement to her interests, or, if the relationship is governed by vague, general standards, then the citizen has a right to a due process procedure to challenge state action.

Traditional property law created a "zone of privacy" or freedom for the individual, protected from arbitrary government action. Reich called for an analogous system of substantive legal entitlements and procedural due protections to govern individual-state relations in the modern social welfare state (Reich; Simon 1983).

The basic paradigm that Reich had in mind, "liberal legalism," stems from classic liberalism. It posits the individual protected by a bundle of legal rights. When the state seeks to regulate the individual's freedom of action, she invokes a legal right and seeks a remedy through procedural due process. The dispute is settled through the "adversary system." Each side presents its case to a disinterested court. The judge decides the case by applying the rule of law—ideally, equally applicable to all regardless of status.

To a large extent, the program that Reich called for did come to pass during the 1960s and mid-1970s. Liberal legalism flourished with the rise of civil rights and spread throughout the legal system. There was a vast outpouring of substantive entitlements and due-process remedies. Health programs were extended to the elderly and the poor; handicapped children were given rights to an "appropriate education"; a wide range of income-maintenance, in-kind, employment, and other social benefits were legislated. Disappointed claimants and recipients had rights to administrative "fair hearings" and judicial review. Many social harms have been converted into protectable legal rights. A few decades ago there were no legal rights, for example, to informed consent in medicine, to special education, to treatment in mental institutions, or to resident protections in nursing homes.

In some important respects, the liberal legal program succeeded. There have been significant changes in our legal culture, our ways of looking at citizens and the state. Many important rights have been defined and improvements have been made. "Rights" talk is now commonplace. Yet, for the most part, the reforms do not work. Most dependent people are not able to take advantage of their rights. When relations are governed by strict rules, they turn out to be oppressive. When relationships are governed by discretion, clients are unable to protect themselves. What went wrong? Why is the system of substantive rights and procedural due process incapable of protecting the individual in the zone of freedom?

Before proceeding with the analysis, it is first necessary to clarify two concepts: autonomy and discretion. The end in the liberal society—the individual that Reich has in mind—is the autonomous, free individual; a principal threat to that individual is discretionary public power. What is the liberal conception of autonomy? How is it compromised by discretion? As we shall see in subsequent chapters, in practice, a great deal of the liberal conception of autonomy is present in communitarian visions, and discretion is an integral part of all of the projects seeking alternatives to liberal legalism.

The Individual in the Zone of Freedom

According to classical liberalism, there cannot be freedom without autonomy. While the concept of autonomy has remained elusive in the philosophical literature (Christman 1988), there is the core idea of self-rule or self-determination. Autonomy is "where the individual determines his or her own course of action in accordance with a plan chosen by himself or herself. The most general idea of autonomy is that of being one's own person, without constraints either by another's action or by a psychological or physical limitation. Both internal and external constraints on action can limit autonomy" (Beauchamp and Childress 1983).

Some insist that autonomy necessarily implies a psychological *capacity* to be self-governing; that is, a person is not autonomous unless equipped with a stable system of values and goals, the ability to understand facts, and a capacity for reasoning, intelligent deliberation, and self-reflection. "It is in light of these capacities that we recognize each other as responsible agents, and this mutual recognition forms the cement of social life" (Connolly 1983:153). There is disagreement, though, on whether autonomy requires rationality. Some argue that there must be a minimal amount of good reasoning, but this implies degrees of autonomy which, in turn, justifies varying degrees of paternalism according to levels of competence. Thus, the rationality requirement is criticized on the grounds that it undercuts the normative requirement that autonomy must be respected equally in all persons insofar as the rationality requirement allows rejection of a person's desires on the basis of reason.

Autonomy requires respect. Gratitude, love, trust, respect, resentment—these are the feelings that arise from the recognition that others have the capacity and responsibility to form intentions and act responsibly, to treat others as people. Connolly argues that it is the reciprocal recognition of these capacities that is the precondition of community (Connolly). Christman, in a recent review of the philosophical literature on autonomy, concludes that, regardless of its ambiguities, autonomy is a fundamental human value that is constitutive of the basic idea of human agency; it has both an intrinsic and an instrumental value (Christman).

Part of the ambiguity in the concept of autonomy arises from its origins in classical liberalism and its use today in the contemporary social welfare state. In its classical context, autonomy or individualism was used to justify free enterprise. The private ownership of property is indispensable to autonomy (Macpherson 1962; Wolff 1968). Liberalism, in this sense, was atomic individualism; each person pursues her self-interest, as free as possible from the constraints or considerations of others. Classical liberalism is concerned with the conditions of independence. In the modern social welfare state, however, the individual is not atomic; she is bound in dense relationships to the state, large bureaucracies, and complex social networks. Hence, autonomy—or, self-determination—is not so much concerned with the conditions of independence as with the conditions of *interdependence*. How can people assert and maintain control over their lives and develop their capacities for growth, love, and respect in their dealings with others? In a recent book, I drew the distinction between classical liberal autonomy and autonomy in *social relations* by use of the term "social autonomy" (Handler 1986).

As used in this book, autonomy—freedom—is a relational concept; it is about the relationship between the agent's desires and some set of constraints. Internal constraints can impede the ability of the actor to deliberate intelligently among alternatives. External constraints limit the ability to act on the choices. Acting freely requires the absence of both kinds of constraints. But these are matters of degree: no one is free from her past or capable of acting without regard to others.

What counts as a constraint? William Connolly draws a distinction in terms of human responsibility. Freedom to act, at the minimum, assumes a natural capacity to act. To name a constraint is to state a grievance against those responsible for it, which excludes barriers not subject to human control. However, Connolly argues for a broad definition of human responsibility; he would not exclude impersonal social forces or draw distinctions between acts of commission or omission. He makes the important point, which will be relevant throughout this book, that ideology plays a role in our construction of social reality, and so-called impersonal forces may be only products of our beliefs. The more dominant the ideology, the more "natural" it seems, and the less likely those who hold these beliefs will think that they are limiting the freedom of others. The assessment of constraints necessarily involves an assessment of underlying beliefs. Constraints on character, especially those that flow from poverty and ignorance, can be profoundly restrictive. These are the constraints that are more likely to be embedded in the structures of our everyday life—work, family, and class. Constraints, as the flip side of freedom, are matters of degree (Connolly).

Discretion

Discretion is ubiquitous, hence difficult to define (Brodkin 1987; Adler and Asquith 1981). Basically, it involves the existence of choice, as contrasted with decisions purportedly being dictated by rules. A common, and useful, example involves law enforcement. The police officer, in assessing an event, exercises choice in determining whether to invoke authority and how much authority; the prosecutor, after weighing the evidence, decides whether to prosecute or not. Similar kinds of choices are available to many regulatory agencies—whether to cite violations or institute other kinds of actions. The opposite scenario would involve situations where the officer feels that there is no choice, that the rules dictate a particular decision. This is a theoretical distinction, and it should not be exaggerated. While it is probably true that in a great many situations officers do feel that they are bound by rules, many important decisions are made by low-level eligibility workers, tax auditors, licensing officials, and other kinds of bureaucrats (Kagan 1984; Lipsky 1980).

Discretion is everywhere in the bureaucracy (Smith 1981; Winkler 1986). Choice has been exercised in the framing of the rules, and quite often, more often than we would like to acknowledge, officials conceal their choices behind the excuse of a rule (Lipsky). In any event, in the relationships that I will be discussing (those involving human service agencies), the distinction is not important; the officials—doctors, social workers, teachers, mental-health workers—have many choices.

Discretion has been attacked on both substantive and procedural grounds. As compared to the idealized version of the rule of law, where parties have equal access and the court applies neutral rules evenhandedly, discretion, it is argued, allows for the bargaining away of publicly defined normative standards and may further disadvantage the weak and the powerless. With regulation, for example, negotiated resolutions will fall short of substantive goals; without procedural protections and the applicability of substantive rights, the poor and weak will be even more victimized by employers, landlords, merchants, and bureaucrats. Bargaining takes place within a normative framework. How are the rules of the game to be maintained? If one party can exploit the rules, there will be an unfair advantage (Abel 1985; Delgado et al. 1985).

The contemporary literature extolling discretion generally ignores distribution issues. Whether arguing for flexibility in regulation, informal justice, or even communitarianism or philosophical dialogism, with few exceptions, it is more or less assumed that the parties are relatively equal; the issue is how the parties can better relate to each other. There has been little systematic consideration of how discretion would work when there are serious inequalities. What are the issues when there are unequal relationships, when a dependent person is dealing with a large-scale public bureaucracy? Discretion gives the official choice. Choice, at least normatively, should be based on a careful weighing of the interests and needs of the client in relation to public considerations. Should this child be placed in this particular special education program? Does this particular applicant qualify for social benefits, and if so, under what conditions? Discretion contemplates a conversation within a normative framework, but dependent people—the poor, minorities, the uneducated, and unsophisticated—are often at a serious disadvantage. They lack the information, the skills, and the power to persuade. The official has the unfair advantage. It is for these reasons that the advocates for the poor and the weak have been so opposed to discretion.

My argument is different. Discretion is inevitable, especially in a great many human-service agencies. It ought to be approached positively and creatively; but ways have to be sought to ensure that power advantages are not exploited, that effective bargaining does in fact take place, and that both parties meaningfully participate in the choices that are to be made.

Before getting to solutions, however, the issues have be examined more closely. Autonomy sets the standard for participation—shared decision-making based on mutual respect. Why are those standards not realized? How is power exercised in the bureaucratic setting? In this chapter, power and participation will be examined sociologically. In Chapters 6 and 7, we will consider structural mechanisms designed to equalize power and maximize the participation of dependent people dealing with bureaucracy.

The Conceptual Flaws in the Liberal Vision: Power and Community

Rather than rely on mutual respect and normative commitments to shared decision-making, the liberal legal program sought to protect people from discretionary decisions through the enactment of clear substantive rights, and where discretion was inevitable, procedural due process protections. But in order for this system to work there has to be a *complaining client.* Our legal system is not proactive. People have to know that they have suffered a harm, they have to blame someone other than themselves, they have to know how to pursue the remedy, they have to have resources to pursue the remedy, and the potential benefits of winning have to outweigh the potential costs. All of these conditions are essential; if there is a failure to negotiate any one condition, then the remedy will fail, the zone of freedom will be penetrated. In general, the legal system fails to protect the dependent person because all of the conditions, almost all of the time, present formidable barriers to dependent people who deal with large-scale public bureaucracies.[1]

There are two major flaws in the liberal legal paradigm as applied to dependent people. Classic liberalism posits the atomic individual warding off intrusions on the zone of freedom. "The New Property," on the other hand, is talking about *continuing relationships*. People and agencies are locked into each other, often for considerable periods of time. Their needs are to resolve their disputes, to repair that relationship, to renew the conversation. The adversary system truncates relationships; there are winners and losers. We find our sharpest criticisms of liberal legalism in those areas where continuity is called for—for example, in custody and neighborhood disputes.

The same criticisms apply to client-agency interactions. Where continuing relationships are required, the costs to the complaining client increase; the relationship may be irreparably damaged, and there is the actual or potential threat of retaliation. The necessity and value of the continuing relationship chill the exercise of rights. Business people who want to keep dealing with each other do not go to law when they have disputes; dependent people lump it (Felstiner, Abel, and Sarat 1980; Macaulay 1963).

When dependent people face bureaucratic systems, their relationships, for the most part, are not governed by tight, closely drawn rules. Rather, they are in discretionary situations. Standards may be loose ("an appropriate education"), or it may be difficult to establish the underlying factual predicates to invoke a rule (for example, financial eligibility, a discriminatory intent), or the service may be inherently discretionary (legal, social, or health services). When the official has discretion, the complaining client only has a right to a hearing, there is no clear answer to the substantive question; who is right or wrong is a judgment call. The law gives the agency the discretion. If the agency acts reasonably—or is careful enough to build a sufficient record—then the court will defer to agency discretion (Handler 1986).

In addition, there is what lawyers call "informal" discretion, activities that social scientists identify as the work patterns of frontline bureaucrats: how they select and sort out clients and otherwise

---

1. These arguments were more fully developed in Handler (1986).

manage their work load. This interaction infects the whole process; it works to raise the barriers initially facing the client in deciding whether to start the process; and it serves to disadvantage the complaining client by controlling information and other resources (Lipsky).

The result is that, in the ordinary case, the bureaucracy wins. In the overwhelming majority of situations, complaints are just not made, and when they are made, clients rarely prevail. Why this happens is revealed when we analyze the exercise of power. This is the second conceptual flaw in liberal legalism: it ignores the distribution question. Relatively powerless people lack the resources to challenge bureaucracies.

Power and the Problem of Quiescence

The standard definition of power is: A has power over B to the extent that he can get B to do something that B would not otherwise do.[2] At first blush, the definition seems unproblematic, especially in the context of the dependent bureaucratic client. The client, as the price of receiving something that is needed, has to do something that the official insists upon—participate in a work program, reveal a matter of privacy, or engage in other kinds of behaviors. The model assumes an objective conflict of interests; there is a direct exercise of power and a knowing, albeit unwilling, submission. The legal rights regime has a response to this situation. If the official acted illegally, then

---

2. While this may be a common and, for our purposes, useful definition of power, there is, in fact, no agreement on the various meanings of power. According to Talcott Parsons, "Power is one of the key concepts in the great Western tradition about political phenomena. It is at the same time a concept on which, in spite of its long history, there is, on analytical levels, a notable lack of agreement both about its specific definition, and about many features of the conceptual context in which it should be placed. There is, however, a core complex of its meaning having to do with the capacity of persons or collectivities 'to get things done' effectively, in particular when their goals are obstructed by some kind of human resistance or opposition." Talcott Parsons, "Power and the Social System," in Steven Lukes (1986:94). The Lukes volume contains a series of essays on various approaches to power. At the end of the introduction, Lukes says: "[I]n our ordinary unreflective judgments and comparisons of power, we normally know what we mean and have little difficulty in understanding one another, yet every attempt at a single general answer to the question has failed and seems likely to fail." Ibid., p. 17.

the dependent person has a right to challenge the exercise of power and a neutral third party will order a remedy.

Suppose, however, that the client willingly submits? Has there been an exercise of power if B *appears* to do what A wants? Now the situation becomes more problematic. What does consent mean in a hierarchical relationship? Can we take the client's position at face value? What other choice do we have? Steven Lukes, in his essay *Power: A Radical View* (1974), addressed the problem of power and quiescence. Lukes argued that there are three dimensions of power. The one-dimensional approach is the example given above, where A gets B to do something he otherwise would not have done. This dimension focuses on observable behavior—"who participates, who gains and loses, and who prevails in decision-making" (Polsby:55). As such, it assumes that grievances and conflicts are recognized and acted upon, that participation occurs within decision-making arenas which are assumed to be more or less open, at least to organized groups, and that leaders, or decision-makers, can be studied as representatives of these groups. Nonparticipation, or inaction, then, is not a political problem; "the empirical relationship of low socio-economic status to low participation gets explained away as the apathy, political inefficacy, cynicism or alienation of the impoverished" (Gaventa 1980:7; Gamson 1968). Quiescence lies in the characteristics of the victims.

The two-dimensional view of power seeks to meet this last point. Bachrach and Baratz argued that power has a "second face" by which it is not only exercised upon the participants within the decision-making arenas but also operates to exclude participants and issues altogether; that is, power not only involves who gets what, when, and how, but also who gets left out and how (Bachrach and Baratz 1962, 1970; Gaventa). Some issues never get on the political agenda—for example, the issue of pollution in a company-dominated town, or the failure of southern Blacks to register and vote prior to the 1965 Voting Rights Act. Apparent inaction is not related to the lack of grievances. Bachrach and Baratz argue that the study of power must also include the barriers to even expressing grievances (Gaventa).

Lukes argues that the two-dimensional view, while a considerable advance, does not go far enough; it fails to account for how power may affect even the *conception* of grievances. The absence of grievances may be due to a manipulated consensus. Furthermore, the dominant group may be so secure that they are oblivious to anyone challenging their position: "the most effective and insidious use of power is to prevent . . . conflict from arising in the first place" (Lukes 1974:23). This is the third dimension of power. A exercises power over B not only by getting him to do what he does not want to do, but "he also exercises power over him by influencing, shaping or determining his very wants" (Lukes 1974:23). Lukes argues this may happen in the absence of observable conflict even though there is a latent conflict between the interests of A and the "real interests" of excluded B.

Molotch and Boden explore the third face of power in an analysis of everyday conversation. They argue that the very grounds of verbal interchange, conversational procedures, act as forms of domination by setting the agenda and determining the outcome (Molotch and Boden 1985). The authors give examples of conversations from people in unequal positions of power and authority—parents, bosses, professors, men.

Demands for "just the facts," the simple answers, the forced-choice response, preclude the "whole story" that contains another's truth. A low structural position carries into conversation a vulnerability to strategies which decrease access to the tacit procedures. . . . The capacity to deprive another of the grounds of talk is founded in a social location that lies outside that particular talk and is reflexively reproduced through it.
Conversations *contain* these power relations in that individuals begin with different capacity to manipulate the tacit procedures and architecture of talk. . . . The result of such a transaction is structural in two senses: the hierarchical nature of the relation among participants is sustained, and the substantive version of reality achieved in common talk is the version offered by the more powerful interactant. Both of these conditions are then external features to the next round of conversation which will . . . again permeate the conditions of interaction. . . . [S]tructure is not something separate from process, but achieved in and through it. (Molotch and Boden:285)

An important characteristic of the third-dimensional view is that it is not confined to looking at the exercise of power in an individualistic, behavioral framework; rather, it focuses on the various ways, whether individual or institutional, by which potential conflicts are excluded. It is much more sociological than either the one- or perhaps the two-dimensional views. Under the third dimension, two theoretical approaches are combined—the hegemonic social and historical patterns identified by Gramsci (1971) and the subjective effects of power identified by Edelman: "Political actions chiefly arouse or satisfy people not by granting or withholding their stable, substantive demands but rather by changing their demands and expectations" (Edelman 1971:8).

The two- and three-dimensional approaches promise to be particularly relevant when considering dependent or relatively powerless people: in the two-dimensional approach, barriers constrain conflict. In the three-dimensional approach, patterns or conceptions of non-conflict preempt manifest conflict (Gaventa).

What are the mechanisms of power in the three dimensions? In the first dimension are the conventional political resources used by political actors: votes, influence, jobs. The second dimension adds what Bachrach and Baratz call the "mobilization of bias." These are the rules of the game—values, beliefs, rituals, as well as institutional procedures—which systematically benefit certain groups at the expense of others. The mobilization of bias operates not only in the decision-making arenas but also, in fact primarily, through "nondecisions" whereby demands are "suffocated before they are voiced, or kept covert; or killed before they gain access to the relevant decision-making arena; or failing all of these things, maimed or destroyed in the decision-implementing stage of the policy process" (Bachrach and Baratz 1970:43). Quiescence can be the product of force or its threat, co-optation, symbolic manipulation, or the silent effects of incremental decisions or institutional inaction (Gaventa).

The mechanisms of power in the third dimension are the least understood. Here is where

> power influences, shapes or determines conceptions of the necessities, possibilities, and strategies of challenge in situations of latent conflict. This may include the study of social myths, language, and symbols, and how they are shaped or manipulated in power processes. It may involve the study of communication of information—both of what is communicated and how it is done. It may involve a focus upon the means by which social legitimations are developed around the dominant, and installed as beliefs or roles in the dominated. It may involve, in short, locating the power processes behind

the social construction of meanings and patterns that serve to get B to act and believe in a manner in which B otherwise might not, to A's benefit and B's detriment. (Gaventa:15–16)

Third-dimensional mechanisms of power include not only the control of information and socialization processes, but also fatalism, self-deprecation, apathy, and the internalization of dominant values and beliefs—the psychological adaptations of the oppressed to escape the subjective sense of powerlessness. Voices become echoes rather than grievances and demands. Behaviors and beliefs interwine. Political consciousness and participation are reciprocal and reinforcing; those who are denied participation will not develop political consciousness. In Paulo Freire's words, because dependent societies are prevented from either participation or reflection, they are denied the very experience necessary for the development of a critical consciousness; instead, they develop a "culture of silence." Moreover, it is the culture of silence which may lend legitimation to the dominant order. Finally, if their voices do emerge, they are especially vulnerable to manipulation by the powerful (Freire 1985; Gaventa).

Gaventa argues that the various mechanisms of power as well as the attributes of powerlessness, in all three dimensions, are interrelated and cumulative; they serve to reinforce each other. Repeated defeats lead to quiescence, which gives the dominant group more opportunity to create barriers of exclusion. The maintenance of power becomes "self-propelled"; thus, "power relationships can be understood only with reference to their prior development and their impact comprehended only in light of their own momentum" (Gaventa:23).

Psychology and Culture

Quiescence has also been analyzed in the disputing literature from the perspective of psychology and culture. Most encounters between field-level officials and clients never give rise to a dispute. In many instances, clients may be satisfied with a decision; in others perhaps only moderately satisfied; and in still other instances, perhaps greatly dissatisfied but still not to the extent that they take action. What does it take to transform an experience or encounter into a dispute? In real life, there is a substantial capacity for people to tolerate considerable distress and even injustice (Felstiner, Abel, and Sarat). The tolerance may be due to a lack of awareness or perception that something wrong is happening to them. Lack of perception may be self-induced or the result of external manipulation.

People may become aware of an injury, but a dispute may still not arise. In order for a dispute to arise, the injured person has to blame someone else (the injured person may blame herself), and even when someone else is blamed, another step is required—that of making a claim or an official appeal to rectify the wrong. A dispute arises when the claim is rejected. The claim may be rejected outright, or it may simply not be acted upon. At this point, nothing more may happen. Clients, for a variety of reasons, may decide to drop the complaint. Or they may decide to pursue whatever remedy is available, for example, a hearing or a lawsuit (Felstiner, Abel, and Sarat).

The antecedents to the formalized dispute are exceedingly important. A great many factors serve to hide the existence of wrongs and injustices or to chill the exercises of claims or modify and alter the form of the claims. A variety of actors—the initial field-level official who made the decision, the advocates who may or may not include professionals, and the listeners, or adjudicators (for example, immediate supervisors)—all serve to filter, discourage, encourage, and alter grievances. Important, too, is the effect of ideology, including changes in the law. Changes in perceptions of rights—"you *can* fight city hall"—remove or diminish an important barrier. On the whole, deep ideological currents serve to justify the status quo, the position of the person in society, the authority and legitimacy of the state, the bureaucracy, and the law (Gordon). It seems self-evident that the poor, minorities, the poorly educated, the newcomer, the frightened, the mentally ill, the sick, and other disadvantaged people are not only more likely to suffer distress and injustice than those better off, but are also less likely to negotiate the antecedents of disputes (Bumiller 1988).

People suffering the same wrongs react differently. Some will recognize the injury, others will not. Some who are aware of the injury will assign blame, others will not. Some will claim while others do nothing. What explains these differences in reaction to similar events? Coates and Penrod (1980–81) used psychological theory to discuss naming, blaming, and claiming in terms of relative deprivation, equity, attribution, and control. People will perceive an injury if they have suffered a *relative* deprivation, when they are treated less favorably than in the past, or in relation to what others are getting. When people feel that they are getting less than others whom they regard as less deserving, they will feel that there is an equity issue, a violation of entitlement. A relative outcome is more important than an absolute one. Comparisons are important in understanding why some people become dissatisfied and not others, despite similar experiences.

Coates and Penrod draw on attribution theory to explain why people differ in drawing conclusions as to the cause of similar experiences—they can either blame themselves or blame others. Self-blame is apparently a forceful human tendency. Studies have shown that the victims of accidents, rape, and spousal violence blame themselves for their misfortunes, even in the face of clearly contrary evidence (Coates and Penrod).

When evidence is ambiguous, people will either tend to forget about the misfortune or reach some kind of explanation through the systematic selection of evidence and personal theories; and here, self-blame becomes an important systematic bias. Once made, attributions tend to have staying power. There is a tendency to stop searching for alternative explanations and new information; instead, people seek out information that confirms the initial bias. The desire to assert some control over events fuels self-blame; it is more comforting than the alternative belief in the power of external forces.

Victims get help in their drive toward self-blame. Both harmdoers and even the uninvolved will often distort information in order to convince themselves that the victims are in some way responsible for the untoward events. Perpetrators will do this for self-justification; observers to convince themselves that somehow they will not suffer the same fate. Thus, both friends and adversaries serve to reinforce the bias of the victim, that the victim is somehow responsible for the misfortune.

Even if there is no self-blame, people still may not do anything. Only certain kinds of external attributions will lead to claiming. If the external cause is considered to be transitory, it is likely no steps will be taken. The harm will disappear rather quickly. Or, the victim may feel helpless and become apathetic, depressed, or seek to escape. People will be more likely to intervene in moderately stable situations, that is, where the harm would continue without some intervention, but there is the possibility that intervention will be successful (Coates and Penrod).

In sum, the forces that serve to suppress and manipulate the complaining capacities of people, especially dependent people, operate at many levels and with varying degrees of subtlety. The liberal legal conception of power and the ability of people to complain is simplistic and naive. But the story is not complete. More specifically, how is power exercised in the social service setting? How do the line officials select, sort, and process clients?

Power in Human Service Agencies

Hasenfeld, in his recent essay "Power in Social Work Practice" (1987), describes the exercise of power in human service agencies from a political economy perspective. The traditional view of social work practice theory is that the client-caseworker relationship is voluntary, mutual, reciprocal, and trusting; traditional theory tends to underestimate unequal power relationships by assuming that, in most relationships, natural power advantages will be neutralized through the voluntary mutuality of interests.

Hasenfeld challenges this view. The principal source of social worker power derives from the resources and services controlled by the agency. Workers are members of organizations, and it is the organizations that determine how their resources are to be allocated. If the clients want these resources, they must yield at least some control over their fate. In addition, workers have other sources of power: expertise, persuasion, and legitimacy. They have specialized knowledge and interpersonal skills.

A great deal of the organizational power is exercised through its standard operative procedures: the type of information that is processed, the range of available alternatives, the decision rules. The agency is concerned with maintaining and strengthening its core activity—the delivery of services. The environment matters; goals represent the interests of those who control the key resources of the agency, which may or may not incorporate professional norms and/ or the interests of the client. In public agencies, which chronically lack the resources to meet demand, social workers are relatively powerless to change the situation; thus, they develop various personal coping mechanisms such as withdrawal and client victimization.

Hasenfeld rejects the concept of mutuality of interests—that agencies and clients share the common goal of helping the client— in favor of a transactional approach. The interests of the client and the agency are determined by their respective systems. Each wants to maximize its own resources while minimizing costs. A person becomes a client to obtain needed resources but tries to do so with a minimum of costs; the social worker needs the resources controlled by the client while minimizing his and the agency's costs. The relationship is governed, then, by the power that each person has over their own interests. Thus, the amount of power that A has over B is a direct function of the resources that A controls and B needs and the inverse function of the ability of B to obtain those resources elsewhere. In short, *"[I]nfluence is synonymous with resources"* (Gamson:93; emphasis original). Agencies that have a monopoly of services exercise considerable power over clients. On the other hand, clients can exercise power if they possess desirable characteristics. Thus, the exchange relationship between the client and the agency can be voluntary or involuntary depending on the degree of choice that each possesses. Furthermore, even in situations where social workers possess considerable power, that power may not necessarily be used. There are rules and regulations, and workers, in varying degrees, are influenced by professional norms and values. But in any event, the traditional social work practice theory assumption of client self-determination is largely untrue for vulnerable groups. There, relationships tend to be involuntary. Moreover, the asymmetrical power relationship between the agency and the client, and hence between the worker and the client, is maintained throughout the structure of social services. The agency is not dependent on the client for its resources. Demand exceeds resources, and most agencies are in monopoly positions. Social workers increase the power advantage through their monopoly of expertise, limiting client access to other workers, making the offer of services conditional on compliance, and limiting options for alternatives.

Agency processes, the structures of discretion, reflect the evaluative criteria of the external funding and legitimating sources. The more powerful the agency, the more it will use its advantages to maintain its position; it will maintain a superior practice and select the more desirable clients. Within the agency, the more powerful workers are better able to control the conditions of their work. In this way, the dynamics of power perpetuate the unequal distribution of quality practice. Poor clients tend to receive poor services. This results not only in an inequality of practice, but, Hasenfeld argues, the practice of inequality.

The distinguishing characteristic of a human service agency is its technology (Hasenfeld 1983). These agencies are designed to change people; thus, the technology not only requires knowledge of the complexities of human behavior, but it must also be a *moral* system. Social service clients are invested with moral and cultural values that define their status. The processes of the organization—intake, intervention, and termination—are crucially shaped by the workers' moral evaluation of the client. Moreover, as clients progress within the system, moral and social attributes change. The technology is based on a conception of human nature, and this conception is reinforced through the selection, processing, and evaluation of the clients.

Because of the inherent uncertainties of the technologies and the demands placed on the workers to respond to demands, the workers develop what Hasenfeld calls *"practice ideologies,"* sets of ideas or ideologies that seek confirmation in self-fulfilling prophecies by screening incompatible information and resisting change or reappraisal. The workers select and deal with those clients that will serve their interests—to confirm their ideologies, comport with the demands of their working conditions, or both. Since technologies and resources are limited, the attributes of the clients who enter are important to organizational success. Thus, organizations seek to attract desirable clients and screen out the undesirable. Although public agencies are often limited in their ability to pick and choose, they employ other mechanisms for acceptance and rejection.

Hasenfeld describes the selection and processing of clients as "typification," which is a pervasive feature in the exercise of field-level discretion. The organization identifies client characteristics in terms of diagnostic labels which then determine the service response.

Agency perceptions of the client's moral character are often determinative. Is the client responsible for her condition and is the client amenable to change? Is the client morally capable of making decisions? Is the client a subject or an object? The answers to these questions, in turn, determine the workers' moral responsibility to the client. The social construction of the client's moral character will have a decisive impact on the treatment that the client receives; thus, the constructed moral character becomes reinforcing.

The mechanism through which the agency delivers the services and gains control over the client is the relationship between the client and the worker. The typical relationship, as described, is one of domination and control. Hasenfeld argues that this relationship is not inevitable; there is an alternative vision—that of equal moral agency. The core of the relationship, according to Hasenfeld, is the nature of the *trust* between the client and the worker. The client has to believe in the desirability of the services and the skill of the worker; the worker has to believe that the client will not abuse the relationship. The worker has to trust the client in order to make the necessary moral commitments. Successful agency intervention depends upon client trust. However, in order for there to be trust, goals and interests have to coincide. There are many barriers to developing a compatibility of interests, but a crucial one, according to Hasenfeld, is the social construction of the client's moral character; simply put, is the client a subject or an object? This theme—trust and equal moral agency as a countervision in bureaucratic relations—will appear throughout the remaining chapters.

The Collapse of the Zone of Freedom

It is now time to draw these various strands together. We have set forth the normative standard for liberalism—autonomy or self-determination. In discretionary contexts, autonomy means shared decision-making based on mutual respect. For dependent people, autonomy has been compromised, if not destroyed, either by the legalization of relationships or the failure of due process. Where discretion has been sharply reduced by rules, as for example in welfare, client behaviors are closely prescribed in massive regulatory codes and are efficiently monitored and enforced through computers. Hierarchy and domination have been consolidated and clients are voiceless.[3]

We see the manifestation of power in discretionary bureaucratic relationships. The three dimensions of power analysis fits the political-economy perspective of social worker-client relations. The first dimension is the paradigm of liberal, legal adversarial relations. A dependent person applies for welfare; a condition of aid is a behavioral change (for example, a work assignment) which the person would prefer not to do, but feels that she must as the price of receiving assistance. Assume that the agency is acting illegally—the person may be legally exempt from the work requirements, the agency may have failed to follow required procedures (e.g., evaluation, offers of training, etc.), or adequate day care was not available. The client knows of the illegality but needs the aid and has no other adequate alternative, but lacks the resources to challenge the agency. Or, the client has available competent legal services and does challenge the agency. This is the first dimension of power: there is an objective event as well as individualized conflict and empirical evidence as to who won what under what circumstances. Power can be defined and measured.

Suppose, however, that the client acquiesces in the condition. Why is there quiescence? Assume that the client is of the same frame of mind—that is, she would prefer not to work. It may be that the agency is acting legally; in this case, the decision has been made legislatively and the agency is not exercising its discretion but is following a rule. The client is now precluded from voicing a grievance, certainly in this forum, but probably in any other arena as well. This would be a case of the second dimension. There is a grievance—the client feels that she unjustly must pay a price for the aid but has been effectively precluded from contesting the decision.

There are other ways in which the second dimension of power can operate. The agency may be operating illegally, and the client feels the grievance but lacks the resources with which to pursue a remedy, or for some other reason feels that it would be either useless or even counterproductive to pursue a remedy. The person may, for

---

3. For a description of how AFDC has been converted from a discretionary to a rule-bound system, much to the detriment of the client, see Handler (1987–88), Simon (1983, 1985, 1986); and Chapter 7.

example, fear retaliation.[4] These are examples of the second dimension of power because even though there is no objectively observed conflict, there is a grievance. Moreover, one could empirically verify not only the grievance, but also the reasons for quiescence. Different client behaviors could be empirically established.

There are also several variations on the third dimension of power—where the absence of conflict is due to a manipulation of consensus, where A shapes and determines the wants of B. The very idea of welfare as an *entitlement* is of recent vintage. Prior to the legal rights revolution of the 1960s, welfare was considered a gratuity, something that was offered on the terms and conditions of the grantor, much as private charity is given today. Given the extremely low level of legal challenges in social welfare programs, one questions even now how far the concept of entitlement has penetrated the consciousness of the disadvantaged (Handler 1986).

Welfare programs have always been concerned about communicating status symbols—those who are worthy, those who are "undeserving" (Himmelfarb). The work requirement is deeply ingrained in American public values—witness the astonishing consensus on work-for-relief today; many think it perfectly normal and appropriate that an applicant for public assistance should work at a public job as the price of the grant; there is very little support for the idea that one is *entitled* to a minimum level of support without any corresponding obligations.[5] To the extent that the applicant for assistance has internalized these values—the obligations of work, responsibility, and welfare—the dominant group has prevented even the conception of the grievance. As Gaventa points out, this view of power is not individualistic; it is much more institutional, more in the nature of the hegemonic social and historical patterns identified by Gramsci and the subjective effects of power discussed by Edelman; power prevents the manifestation of conflict at all. The poor have been socialized into believing that there is no entitlement to a minimal standard of living without a corresponding obligation to work.

The social and historical patterns and the subjective effects iden-

---

4. For a discussion of the barriers to exercising rights to administrative fair hearings, see Handler (1986).
5. Even Heidi Hartmann (1987) and Lawrence Mead (1986) agree on work requirements. For a discussion of the current consensus on work and welfare reform, see Handler (1987–88).

tified by Gramsci and Edelman are, of course, much more deeply rooted, much more pervasive than even the complex example of welfare and the work obligation. They are manifest in many of the relationships between the dependent citizen seeking services or trying to avoid sanctions and the officer who controls the resources. Both the powerful and the powerless carry into the relationship their respective characters and self-conceptions, their root values, nurtured through immediate as well as past social relationships. Who they are and where they come from—class, race, childhood, education, employment, relations with others, the everyday structures of their lives, their very different social locations—crucially affect their languages, social myths, beliefs, and symbols; how they view themselves, their world, and others produce vastly different meanings and patterns in their encounters. What is the staff professional's self-perception and view of the person sitting across the desk? What is the client's self-perception and view of the person sitting opposite? It is no surprise that in social welfare situations clients either fail to pursue their grievances or fail even to conceptualize a grievance. The structures of their social lives shape their identities and direct their behavior (Molotch and Boden).

The collapse of the liberal legal vision sets the stage for the subsequent analysis. Bureaucratic law has penetrated the zone of freedom of dependent clients and has destroyed their capacity for self-determination. Habermas calls this phenomenon the "colonization of the lifeworld" (Chapter 4). From various quarters, including jurisprudence, sociology, and moral philosophy, the search is for principles and practices that will restore and preserve self-determination in relationships.

Self-Determination in Health Care: An Alternative Vision?

Is there an alternative? Can there be self-determination in dependent relations? This book argues that there can be. To end this chapter and introduce later themes, I offer the vision of shared decision-making that exists in one of the most traditional hierarchical discretionary relationships—that between physician and patient. The idea that freedom and autonomy can exist in medical decision-making has been articulated by the President's Commission for the Study of Ethical Problems in Medicine and Biomedical and Behavioral Research (1983). Informed consent in medicine is an important example.

The traditional physician-patient relationship is characterized by great disparities in information and power: the professional knows best; the "good" patient is one who follows doctor's orders; and the legal requirements of informed consent have been distorted into a ritualistic exercise designed to avoid malpractice liability. The opposite standard is genuine participation in joint decision-making. The commission states that ethically valid consent is a process of shared decision-making based upon mutual respect and participation. In order for there to be full participation, there must be mutual respect. According to the commission, there are two ethical foundations for its standard of informed consent—personal well-being and self-determination.

Under traditional medical paternalism, the physician had both the right and the responsibility to make decisions in the best medical interests of the patient. The opposite case, maximum patient sovereignty, would have patients accept full responsibility for and control over all decisions about their care. Physicians would only transmit medical information and use their technical skills at the direction of the patients. Both positions are wrong, according to the commission, because they attempt to vest exclusive moral agency, ethical wisdom, and decision-making authority on one side, and leave the other side in a dependent role. Patient choice is not absolute; it is limited by acceptable professional practice and the provider's own ethical values as well as available health care resources.

The commission envisions a broad-ranging, evolving, and dynamic conversation between physician and patient. The personalities, characters, attitudes, and values of the participants are essential components of the process. The process is flexible and dynamic; decisions are subject to reconsideration and modification as circumstances change. The physician invites the patient to participate in a dialogue in which the professional seeks to help the patient understand the medical situation and available courses of action, and the patient conveys her concerns and wishes.

The commission believes that the ethical value of patient well-being will be enhanced through this process. There is a great deal of uncertainty in medicine, and decisions often reflect the physician's, and not necessarily the patient's, values. But the patient's reasonable subjective preferences are material. Well-being depends on the patient's needs and on what the patient thinks she wants; this is an individual, specific matter. Shared decision-making requires that the physician seek to understand the needs of each patient and present alternatives so that the patient can make known preferences. There must be a physician-patient dialogue to clarify views.

The other ethical value specified in the commission's report is self-determination, the commission's term for autonomy. Self-determination, generally, is the individual's exercise of the capacity to form, revise, and pursue personal life plans. Self-determination in health care is an instrumental benefit: under most circumstances, it will promote well-being. But there is also an intrinsic value to self-determination, as it acts as both a shield and a sword. It protects individuals from the outside control; it also creates self-agency. Individuals become subjects, not objects. They define their own characters, taking responsibility for their personhood. The choice is theirs to make.

Self-determination is not absolute. It is limited by public policy or the interests of others. Individual decision-making can also be so defective or mistaken that it fails to promote the person's own interests or goals. Thus, decisions can be overridden to promote the person's other goals of well-being. However, the commission argues that decision-making capacity must be judged in terms of the particular decision rather than either the person's *status* or the *content* of the decision. Decisions about capacity must be based on the person's actual functioning in the specific context. When capacity is unclear, it must be evaluated over time in order to assess the patient's understanding of information and reasoning.

In the commission's view, capacity consists of the following: (1) a set of reasonably stable values or goals; (2) the ability to communicate and understand information; and (3) the ability to reason and deliberate about one's choices.

It is not easy to determine capacity. Virtually all conscious adults can perform some tasks but not others. For the particular decision, the patient must have the ability to understand the relevant facts and alternatives, to consider the decision within a framework of values and goals; she must be able to reason, deliberate, and give reasons for the decision in light of the facts, the alternatives, and its impact on the person's own goals and values.

The degree to which people possess or exercise these abilities may vary. For example, they may lack a sufficient reasoning capacity or understanding of the facts. Efforts have to be made, then, to improve those aspects of their decision-making capacities. The commission rejects the "express preference" standard—that is, the expression of a preference about a treatment decision that demonstrates capacity or a test that looks solely at the content of the decision. "The practitioner's belief that a decision is not 'reasonable' is the beginning—not the end—of an inquiry into the patient's capacity to decide" (President's Commission:62).

Consent that is substantially involuntary lacks a moral basis for treatment; it does not respect the patient's dignity and may not reflect the aims of the patient. Voluntariness, however, is a matter of degree. People can be coerced or subtly manipulated. In the medical area, blatant coercion is usually not a problem because it is usually so easy for a physician to use more subtle means. The physician's ability to package and present the facts can leave the patient with no real choice. The manner in which information is presented is affected by the disparities in knowledge, position, and influence between physician and patient. Many patients, in medical situations, are fearful, and unequal in status, knowledge, and power, and are, thus, particularly susceptible to subtle manipulations through the physician's careful choice of words, nuances of tone, and emphasis.

There is considerable evidence, however, that proper communication is therapeutic. There are many circumstances under which patients are knowledgeable about their conditions and, as a result of involvement in the decision-making process, are likely to emerge in better health. A number of studies show that informed patients are more likely to comply with therapeutic regimes, have reduced levels of anxiety, recover faster from surgery, and have enhanced ability to protect their own well-being by detecting errors and recognizing untoward side effects. In addition, patients who make their own decisions are more likely to be able to better advance their life plans.

It has also been found that having information and understanding its implications increases patient self-confidence. Educated patients tend to feel more competent about managing their illnesses and freer to interact with the medical staff. Presenting information in a way that maximizes understanding is a prerequisite for more equal participation. On the other hand, for messages to be understandable, professionals must be clear in their own minds about what information is most important. This process of self-scrutiny is most important, and may have the additional benefit of causing physicians to rethink, or at least review, their own diagnosis, prognosis, and recommendations (President's Commission).

We will return to this example in Chapter 6, where we consider other specific examples of self-determination. The concept is introduced here to specify what freedom and autonomy *can* look like in the modern state. Self-determination, as in medical ethics, is relational. But even though dependent people are in discretionary relationships, that relationship does not have to be dominating and oppressive.

Chapter 3
Regulation and Organization

This chapter discusses three literatures usually not considered together: the critique of contemporary regulation; informal justice or alternative dispute resolution; and the sociology of organizations. All three literatures describe in various ways the structure of power. The legal, scientific, and policy analyses in the three literatures describe what happened to the legal rights project at the hands of the bureaucracy. The characteristics of bureaucracy are central. The regulation and informal justice literatures explicitly call for a restructuring of bureaucracy that would pull back the reach of the state and allow for more flexibility and communication of the parties at the field level; this would provide the space and incentives for more autonomous and communitarian relationships (themes which are discussed at a more theoretical level in Chapter 4). The sociology of organizations serves two purposes, providing a sociological perspective for both the regulation and informal justice literature reviewed in this chapter as well as the jurisprudential themes in the next chapter. The calls for reform throughout this book ultimately filter through bureaucracy.

Regulatory Unreasonableness

The "crisis" in regulation is that too many aspects of society, and especially the economy, are overregulated. There are too many regulations; they are too detailed, technical, and legalistic. As a result, contemporary regulation is dysfunctional: unnecessary costs are imposed on industry, innovation is stifled, and regulatory goals are not accomplished. The crisis is typically discussed at two levels—internally, within the regulatory program itself, and at the level of system failure where, in a complex modern society, various regulatory systems or fields fail to mesh and thus work at cross-purposes.

The theoretical and empirical literature on regulation contrasts two competing styles. The first style, usually called "command and control," is concerned with the application of punishment for specific violations; the decision-making process is adversarial and relies on legal machinery. The second style is concerned with conciliation and accommodation, focusing on prevention rather than punishment: while regulators respond to a particular problem, the emphasis is on negotiating future conformity; the decision-making process is often private and informal (Hawkins 1984).

Liberal ideology and politics favor command-and-control regulation: it is based on the positive law; it is visible, universal, and equal in treatment. Conciliation, accommodation, bargaining, and flexibility are nevertheless always present; bargaining is tolerated because of necessity, but it is not celebrated. At times the courts ignore this "informal discretion"; at other times, they attempt to confine it or structure it (Shapiro). What is new today, in the literature, is the change of attitude toward the bargaining style of regulation. The scholarly literature not only recognizes the importance of this countervision, but argues for its legitimacy and more widespread application.

What gives rise to the bargaining style of regulation and why is it problematic? It is in the area of field-level enforcement that the case for and against informal, flexible regulation is most clearly made. The most popular example is criminal law enforcement, where prosecutorial discretion and plea bargaining have long been acknowledged and legitimated; police discretion is also well known, but far more problematic. Not many are happy with discretion in the criminal law. It is considered to be necessary to avoid a complete breakdown of the criminal justice system, but this conclusion has been sharply challenged (Schulhofer 1984).

In the area of economic and social regulation, one of the prime targets is the Occupational Safety and Health Administration

(OSHA). Bardach and Kagan, in their book *Going by the Book: The Problem of Regulatory Unreasonableness*, present the case against OSHA. The real explosion in protective regulatory law came in the 1960s and early 1970s when there was increased knowledge and intolerance of the risk of being cheated, or of suffering harm in the environment, the workplace, or from products. There were also changes in our legal culture. The legal rights revolution spread from minorities and the poor to the economy. "[S]ocial harms were characterized as violations of moral rights, automatically to be converted into protectable legal rights" (Bardach and Kagan 1982:13). The violation of a "right" became a "wrong"; and responsibility for correcting or avoiding that wrong shifted from the individual to society or business. During this period, protective regulatory law was good politics. There were other reasons for the expansion. It is well known that special-interest groups often use regulatory law to improve their competitive position. Regulatory bureaucracies also seek to expand their domain. Then, particular events such as scandals, scientific discoveries, and most significantly, catastrophes fuel the demand for more regulation.

Regulation tends to increase, but why, ask Bardach and Kagan, does it tend to become unreasonable? Regulations tend to be overinclusive. Laws are universalistic; they apply to all business of a particular type regardless of variation; and the norms of equal treatment push toward uniform application, producing what the authors call on-site unreasonableness (Ackerman and Stewart 1985; Bardach and Kagan; Steiner 1983). At the same time, there has been an increasing legalization of enforcement. Statutes, regulations, and court decisions have become increasingly specific, discretion has been narrowed, and enforcers more concerned with the legality of their actions (Steiner). The changes were designed to make the program tougher.

There are strong pressures for the legalistic approach. Businesses want the security of precision and the certainty that their competitors are not getting an advantage through some secret bargain. Inspectors like the security of quantitative measures of performance. Detailed rules give the appearance of fairness, uniformity, and the absence of corruption; difficult judgment questions can be avoided and higher authority can be invoked in a hostile field environment. Nevertheless, legalistic regulation often results in delays, defeats on technicalities, or, at least in the view of the field staff, weak sanctions. Formal legal challenges are costly to the agency; there are massive information-gathering burdens (Ackerman and Stewart); and often agencies seek to avoid aggressive challenges. In many agencies, a formal proceeding is rare (Hawkins 1986).

Unreasonableness arises not only because of variety in the real world but also because of the numerous ways in which violations may occur. It is a mistake, argue Bardach and Kagan, to think that all violations occur from deliberate attempts to evade the law. Rather, many come about through incompetence, carelessness, lack of supervision, lack of knowledge, or accidents. Yet, we view accidents as industrywide problems caused by insufficient regulation and which require industrywide solutions. Problems are exaggerated; solutions are simplistic; and the costs of regulatory solutions are ignored. Because we either lack understanding of causation or cannot get to it through regulation, we use proxies—for example, staffing ratios in health care, warning signs, records and procedures—which are easily monitored but are only marginally useful.

Bardach and Kagan claim that good inspectors can quickly tell a good situation from a bad one, they know how to be flexible, and when to work with a person. They know the territory. But this kind of enforcement is no longer allowed. It looks too much like capture. Today, good enforcement is one that is consistent, has a sufficiently high citation rate, and does not bargain. Inspectors, say Bardach and Kagan, are now concerned with violations and citations; they are not concerned with solving problems, they have been turned into cops.

Regulation, even tough regulation, has many values; but what it cannot get at is the attitudes of responsible people. Rules cannot cover everything; compliance needs agreement and cooperation. Yet, in the opinion of the authors, tough regulation is perverse. Instead of fostering cooperation, it destroys it. By emphasizing violations rather than problems and the necessity to cite all violations, regulation creates bitterness and adversariness. Everything must be put on the record. Businesses will not share information; agencies are subject to charges of collusion if they receive information confidentially. A "culture of resistance" sets in. Strict standards and strict enforcement, it is claimed, waste huge amounts of money and resources, discourage innovations, and result in massive counterproductive litigation (Ackerman and Stewart; Rabin 1986; Rose-Ackerman 1988).

While OSHA is usually cited as the prime example of the pathologies of command-and-control regulation, it is by no means unique. A great deal of environmental, consumer, and other kinds of social regulation is also criticized on this ground (Ackerman and Stewart; Steiner). One of our examples in Chapter 6 is long-term care for the frail elderly poor; the critique of nursing home regulation follows the same analysis as Bardach and Kagan (Vladeck 1980).

What would the opposite style of regulation look like? Keith Hawkins thinks that, despite the public insistence on prosecution-deterrence, the conciliatory style is more the norm. In part, this is because of the behavior that is to be controlled. The legalistic approach works best where the conduct is discrete and there is no basis for a continuing relationship. But where conduct is continuous, more in the nature of states of affairs than discrete acts, then it is a "problem." Problems are amenable to correction over time (Hawkins 1984; 1986).

Hawkins studied water pollution control at the field level in two large districts in England. There, the enforcement agents initially rely on negotiation. Although it is always in the background, prosecution is rarely used; in fact, it is regarded as a sign of failure by the agency. The social context of water pollution control is ambivalent. Environmental and health concerns compete with demands of economic activity. And, although sometimes conduct is clearly blameworthy, more often pollution is the result of accidents. The ambivalence is reflected in the posture of the agency and in the generally low level of sanctions. Mediating between strict laws are judgments of blameworthiness that are shared by both the agency and the industry. Sanctions are imposed when violations are deliberate or, if negligent, are accompanied by uncooperativeness; in other words, if the firm challenges the authority and legitimacy of the agency. Enforcement is always less a reflection of the law and more a reflection of agency concepts of self-preservation.

Field-level enforcers insist on relatively few "consent" conditions which are clear and attainable, and they then ensure that these are complied with. They concentrate on the major problems, figuring that small problems will be taken care of. The agents give warnings, advice, information, and consultation. The emphasis is on surveillance and prevention. They seek to preserve good relations or build new ones. They need easy access to property and information and the ability to raise sensitive issues. It is not unusual for dischargers to self-report, which means, in effect, that the act will normally not be penalized. If the polluter has the right attitude, compliance may proceed by increments. If the infraction has been corrected, the agency considers prosecution to be wasteful and vindictive.

The agency does prosecute from time to time, but it does so for symbolic reasons—to demonstrate that it is enforcing the law and to keep alive its credibility. The agency carefully selects a small number of important but winnable cases. But the main goal of regulation is to secure change, not punishment, and to this end, negotiation is the preferred strategy.

Hawkins argues that the cooperative or compliance style of regulation is pervasive. It is rooted in *reciprocity*—the agency bargains on the less serious offenses, treats the regulated with respect, exchanges information, is responsive to the problems of compliance, and is considerate of good faith. Forbearance is offered for compliance. The agency achieves regulatory goals at less cost.

The above studies describe a cooperative style of regulation at the field level. Other scholars argue that this style should be extended farther back in the administrative process—to the policy- and rule-making stages (Shapiro 1983). Negotiation, bargaining, mediation, and arbitration would then replace traditional adjudication and rule-making procedures. An example of this cooperation would be where the Environmental Protection Agency, the firms, and other interested parties negotiate a standard for emissions. The purported advantages include the introduction of flexibility and a mix of incentives to encourage what Richard Stewart calls both "market innovation" and "social innovation" (improved products and processes that will reduce externalities). He says that the present legalistic system discourages both types of innovation. Other advantages include reducing uncertainty, delay, and the costs of compliance, eliminating or reducing special burdens on new products, and reducing the effects of a cumbersome and inefficient decisional process (Stewart).

Of course, there are a number of concerns about negotiated rule-making (Shapiro and McGarity 1989): Who is included in the negotiations? How can we be sure that the agency is not being too passive or co-opted? What about regulatory "entitlements"—for example, a worker's right to a "safe workplace"? In much of the literature on the compliance style, there is little discussion of the victims—workers, consumers, those exposed to environmental hazards (Abel 1985; Noble 1986; Silbey 1980–81; Shapiro 1983). Other critics think that the bargaining approach will tend to preserve the status quo; it will favor those who already are in powerful positions and will disfavor a reconsideration of current paradigms (Winter 1985).

There is great unease about the compliance style. Part of that unease is rooted in the tensions between the symbols of command-and-control regulation and the inevitable need for discretion. No enforcement agency can enforce all of the law all of the time; there has to be discretion. But we worry about corruption and capture. There is concern that the costs of formal proceedings are used to bargain away regulatory goals, or that the enforcing agency will be able to override procedural requirements designed to protect the weak in formal proceedings (Harrington 1988; Latin 1985).

Critics of negotiated approaches are usually concerned about the failure to achieve regulatory goals. The agency's basic chip is to refrain from exercising its full authority in order to reduce compliance costs and decisional costs. But this is not necessarily true. There are situations where agencies demand behavior that is at the border of their authority. This, of course, is an old practice in land-use, where agencies extract something "extra" from the developers; the contemporary version involves "linkages" whereby cities press for minority contracts and employment.[6] What is new to the practice is the discourse—the recognition and defense of bargaining (Winter).

Does it necessarily follow that the compliance strategy will result in the failure of regulatory goals? According to Robert Axelrod, no. In *The Evolution of Cooperation* (1984), he has developed a theoretical model, based on game theory, which demonstrates that, under

---

6. Some aspects of this practice are now constitutionally suspect. *City of Richmond v. J.A. Crosen Co.*, 109 S.Ct.706 (1989).

certain circumstances, cooperation can be based on self-interest, and both parties can be better off. The key point is the difference between a finite and an infinite number of encounters; in the former, there is no incentive to cooperate, but cooperation can begin to emerge when the players know that they have to deal with each other in the future. Each actor then has to take account of the other's strategy. Cooperation is based on reciprocity. Axelrod's principles (or advice) for fostering cooperation remarkably track the empirical practices of the water pollution control inspectors: (1) don't think in terms of zero-sum, for in nonzero-sum, one does not have to do better than the other and both can succeed (in fact, one's success is a prerequisite for the other's); (2) don't be the first to "defect" (i.e., take advantage of the other); the best predictor of success is the actor who was "nice"; (3) reciprocate both cooperation and defection; and (4) clarity.

Hawkins's inspectors and firms were better off cooperating—information was exchanged and regulatory goals were accomplished at less cost; inspectors would give firms the benefit of the doubt if they displayed the proper attitude; but there would be swift escalation if the firm challenged the agency. The relationship worked best when there were a few clearly stated conditions that focused on important infractions. Axelrod insists that cooperation is not really founded on trust but on the importance of the enduring relationship, on utility maximization rather than altruism. Deterrence and compliance strategies are not necessarily mutually inconsistent; in fact, they can co-exist depending on the circumstances (Scholz 1984; compare Boyd and Loberbaum 1987).

Scholars have presented alternatives to command-and-control regulation which, they claim, can accomplish regulatory goals more efficiently and, at the same time, enhance democratic values of participation. Bruce Ackerman and Richard Stewart would modify the existing permit system under the Clean Air Act by auctioning pollution permits and allowing polluters to buy and sell each other's permits (Ackerman and Stewart). Polluters with high clean-up costs would purchase permits from those with low costs. These two reforms, the authors claims, would encourage innovation and transfer the information tasks from the overburdened agency to the managers and engineers. To implement such a system, the agency would have to do four things: (1) estimate the level of pollution in each watershed and air quality region; (2) establish an efficient auction system whereby polluters can regularly buy pollution rights for limited terms; (3) establish a title registry in each region where buyers and sellers could transfer rights; and (4) consistently penalize polluters who exceed their permits.

These reforms would create a quite different regulatory regime. The agency would no longer be required to determine, through costly adversary techniques, the best available technology for each major industry in the United States and to defend these determinations in court. Officials would no longer be required to consider endless adaptations to changing local conditions of every significant source of pollution. Instead, local managers and engineers would be able to determine their own costs, and either sell or buy permits as required. The permits would be for a fixed term, after which the polluters would be required to buy new permits in each watershed and air quality control region. This system will also encourage the agency to monitor more diligently; permits are valuable only if there is strict enforcement. Enforcement disputes would concentrate on whether or not the polluter exceeded its permits rather than on complex technology issues. Ackerman and Stewart claim that the EPA has already instituted some of these reforms, with considerable success, under its "bubble" and "trade-off" programs.

Would such a program compromise policy goals? Not necessarily, argue the authors. The debate would shift from arcane technology issues to overall questions dealing with levels of pollution versus other societal goals such as development and employment. Moreover, the authors would urge Congress to focus on average levels, and allow the agency flexibility in terms of regions and ecological and economic variations (Ackerman and Stewart).[7]

Susan Rose-Ackerman sketches a similar kind of approach for OSHA regulation. Assuming that there are trade-offs between health and safety provisions on the one hand, and employment levels, the real value of take-home pay, and product prices on the other, she argues that it is not self-evident that workers are always better off with higher health and safety standards. Instead of the present

---

7. For a recent evaluation of this policy, giving a guarded, mixed review, see Hahn and Hester (1989).

command-and-control regime, she proposes that information be improved by requiring employers to inform workers and job applicants of risks in clear and nontechnical form and that government sponsor research on risk levels. She then proposes a two-tiered regulatory scheme: The first level would encompass minimal, serious risks enforced by strict requirements which cannot be bargained away. More stringent standards would be covered by the second tier and would be bargained between employers and employees (either individually or through their unions). These standards would only be relaxed in exchange for job-related benefits. There would be protections for workers who asserted rights under this scheme. Other scholars also call for more flexibility in OSHA (Shapiro and McGarity).

In all of these proposals, there are certain common themes. A principal one is the desire to pull back the reach of strict regulation and create space within which the interested parties can adjust relationships to particular circumstances. At the field level, in the everyday world, circumstances are varied and adjustments have to be made to achieve both regulatory goals and economic efficiency. The legal-bureaucratic regulatory regime is too intrusive, too clumsy. It cannot function at this level of detail; it is overburdened and inadequate. As a result, it distorts the market system. Neither regulatory goals nor efficiency is achieved.

But these authors are not abandoning regulatory goals and calling for a return to the free market. Rather, they are searching for appropriate roles for regulation and the market, where each system can function properly—not independently, but in a relationship that reaches a better accommodation between regulatory goals and economic efficiency (Steiner). They look at the strengths and weaknesses of each system and ask how can they mesh for a better balance between policy goals and economic efficiency. While this point is sharply contested (Harrington 1988; Latin), all of the authors claim that policy goals will be better served by a better accommodation. We will return to this theme in the next chapter when we consider Continental theories of reflexive law and the jurisprudence of Niklas Luhmann and Jürgen Habermas. They claim that regulatory regimes have colonized other social systems with serious dysfunctional results; they also argue that the regulatory system has to pull back so that there is space for other systems to function in terms of their own sociological demands.

There is another theme in these proposals that is emphasized by some of the scholars and implied by the others. Axelrod, Bardach, Kagan, and Hawkins, in various ways, stress the relevance of personal relationships, individual needs and circumstances, motives, and attitudes; and the idea that command-and-control regulation stifles these considerations, whereas the cooperative style of regulation fosters them. Hawkins's inspectors and managers talk and listen to each other, take into account their needs, and make their bargains in light of individual circumstances and agency goals. All of the scholars emphasize the importance of generating and exchanging reliable information. Bargaining, in these situations, is a dialogue, and a dialogue implies autonomy, self-determination; there is listening as well as talking. This is a major theme in the next section, which deals with informal justice, as well as in the chapters that deal with jurisprudence and ethical philosophy.

Informal Justice

The explosion of legal rights and the expansion of regulatory law were bound to produce a reaction. Critics feared that the granting of procedural due process would swamp the hearing process in social welfare. In the regulatory area, it was feared consumers and environmentalists would cause irreparable delay and stifle innovation in the American economy through the use of formal administrative proceedings. There arose the alarm that we were in the grip of a litigation crisis (Galanter 1983). In economic regulation, the call was for deregulation. There also arose a renewed and expanded interest in "informal justice"—mechanisms that would process disputes outside of, or as an alternative to, formal procedures—such as community boards, neighborhood justice centers, and mediation and arbitration (Harrington and Merry 1983).

Part of the informal justice impulse derived from the social activism of the 1960s, which demanded greater substantive justice and procedural flexibility. This was a period of antiprofessionalism: there were demands for lay or client participation and the extension of dispute resolution processes in the workplace, the neighborhood, and the family. The other source of the impulse came from the establishment side—the American Bar Association, then–Chief

Justice Burger, large law firms, insurance and commercial companies. They sought to manage disputes better so that they could clear congested court dockets and decide claims more efficiently, quickly, and inexpensively (Rosenberg 1986).

There are a variety of informal institutions, and it is difficult to draw boundaries or develop a working concept of what are the formal or informal sectors. According to Richard Abel, most of the informal institutions that deal with "minor" disputes display at least some of the following characteristics: they are structurally nonbureaucratic, or at least far less bureaucratic than the organizations that they purport to be substitutes for; they tend to be undifferentiated from the larger society; they minimize the use of professionals; and they favor substantive and procedural norms that are vague, particularistic, flexible, and commonsensical. The common enemy of these informal institutions is formalism (Abel 1982). On the other hand, one also finds fairly structured "informal" mechanisms operating within even more highly structured institutions—for example, court-sponsored summary jury trials as an alternative to the full trial. In terms of formal characteristics, one finds today a continuum of dispute-processing institutions rather than sharp demarcations among them (Bush).

Whatever the difficulties in defining boundaries, alternative dispute resolution—as it is now popularly called—has caught on. This is not to say that today more cases are being settled before trial than before; this has been true of all times, and it is hard to show empirically what trends have occurred. We do know that more than ninety percent of all civil and criminal trials are settled before trial. But what is new today is the recognition and endorsement of the phenomenon. Alternative dispute resolution has a respected academic and scholarly title; it has foundation support; and, as will be discussed shortly, it has the active embrace of the judiciary. Alternative dispute resolution is the norm; formal adjudication is the exception (Menkel-Meadow 1986).

The juvenile court, the small claims court, and housing courts are early examples of institutions where disputes were supposed to be handled less formally and less professionally, but more quickly and inexpensively. During the 1970s, attention was paid more to counterinstitutions, such as community boards, neighborhood justice centers, and other kinds of lay decision-making bodies. What is perhaps most interesting today is the movement of structures and ideologies toward informal dispute resolution that is taking place in the most formal structures of all—the courts. Increasingly, courts are adopting arbitration that includes the active participation of the judge. At the present time, ten United States District Courts and more than fifteen states provide court-annexed arbitration as an alternative to the court process. The arbitration process is obligatory but not binding. If one of the parties disagrees, the case then goes to court and there is no reference to the arbitration. Other devices used by the courts include summary jury trials (impaneling a jury to hear an abbreviated version of the case) and referrals (Bush 1989; Rosenberg).

What is leading this drive toward alternative dispute resolution? Part of the answer is efficiency. Alternative dispute resolution promises a more rational allocation of dispute-processing resources. Initially, the idea was to clear the court dockets of "little" cases or the very large, complex case; but now, a major consumer of alternative dispute resolution is commercial litigation. Another theme of alternative dispute resolution is community empowerment through self-government. Other motives include extending social control through the expansion of the "therapeutic state" or creating second-class justice for the lower social classes (Abel 1982; Delgado 1985; Harrington and Merry). But the area that I am interested in, as a matter of theory, is the substantive motive—that the informal system will provide better justice—that the citizen will be spared unnecessary expense and stress, that the process will be more appropriate, and, most important, that the remedies will be more adequate (Rosenberg).

Whether mediation and settlement will produce better substantive results than adjudication may depend on the style of the process. "Bargaining in the shadow of the law" can reproduce adversarial relationships in its own setting. Carrie Menkel-Meadow describes the differences between adversarial negotiation and "problem-solving" negotiation. In the adversarial style, as in adjudication, there are "winners" and "losers." Each party wants as much as she can get, and the more that one wins, the other loses. The prescribed tactics are withholding as much information as possible, stating high demands in anticipation of reducing them if necessary, and trying to take advantage of one's "opponent" through tactical maneuvers (e.g., negotiating in one's own office; assuming responsibility for drafting the agreement) (Menkel-Meadow 1984).

The adversarial style of negotiation is predicated on a simple view of reality—for example, that the buyer wants the lowest price, the seller the highest, that each dollar is worth the same for each of the parties. While this may be true for some situations, most such zero-sum relationships are rare in real life. Usually there are multiple issues and, thus, room for trade-offs.

Adversarial negotiation also assumes that the parties value resources in the same manner. However, frequently price is not the only issue; there are matters of quantity, quality, and delivery. By assuming that the subject of negotiations is fixed, the parties often miss the opportunity to expand the resources that may become available and they may fail to consider the full range of their opponents' needs.

"Compromise" is the key word ... in the descriptions of what settlement conferences are supposed to encourage. Compromise is a problematic term, connoting the necessity for both parties to give something up and reach an agreement "in the middle." Settlements do not necessarily result in compromise, and the settlement officer who begins by pushing for a compromise has already severely limited what may be achieved. (Menkel-Meadow 1985:485, n. 3)

Menkel-Meadow urges a "problem-solving" model of negotiation. The assumptions of the model are that the parties typically have underlying needs or objectives and that, although relief asked for is usually money, monetary relief may be a proxy for other things. By uncovering the underlying needs, opportunities are presented for more numerous and better-quality solutions which, moreover, may not be mutually exclusive. This possibility exists because people do not have the same values. The task of the parties is to search for "complementary interests." Rather than assuming the other party's needs (adversarial negotiation), both sides must actively determine what the needs of both parties are in fact. Multiple needs lead to flexibility. Moreover, these needs will change over time.

The styles of the two methods differ in practice. In adversarial negotiations, the parties will argue, often fruitlessly, about the facts and the law—they are in the shadow of the court, which will decide who is right and who is wrong. In problem-solving, there is less need to focus on these issues, and there is less need to withhold information. Rather, problem-solving emphasizes clarification and communication: it is future-oriented.

Menkel-Meadow does not argue that problem-solving is *the* solution for all disputes. What she does argue is that it is potentially more useful for many life situations that are falsely characterized as zero-sum. By looking at the future in terms of multiple needs and objectives rather than hopelessly trying to reconstruct the past, parties have the opportunity to be creative. It is a cooperative strategy. While Menkel-Meadow doubts that the efficiency claim for settlement has been proved, she is persuaded that substantive justice and substantive process are more likely to be achieved through problem-solving settlement processes (Menkel-Meadow 1985).

The problem-solving method of negotiation seems a fairly accurate description of the example posed by Hawkins's water pollution control inspectors. Hawkins described an exploration of underlying needs for both the firm and the agency. By forbearing on prosecution and forgiving minor infractions, the firm can comply at a lower cost, the plant manager has an incentive to search for the most cost-effective methods of compliance, and, by complying, the firm helps the agency achieve regulatory goals at lower costs. In Menkel-Meadow's terms, there is a mutual exploration of needs and a search for creative solutions where both parties are better off.

Much of alternative dispute resolution is instrumental. It is designed to resolve conflicts more efficiently, but also with better substantive results for the parties. There are, however, larger or deeper normative claims made about alternative dispute resolution—both negative and positive. On the negative side, there are serious concerns that the disadvantaged will suffer even more under regimes of informal justice. However badly the poor and minorities may fare in the formal justice system, they do have legal rights and are offered at least the pretense of evenhanded justice. And, on occasion, rights are vindicated. The argument is that even these slim protections will be lost in informal justice. As stated in Chapter 2, a fundamental flaw in the legal rights paradigm is the failure to take account of the maldistributions of wealth and power. Much of the informal justice literature does not address this same underlying issue; the poor, minorities, women, and other disadvantaged people are still in the same position, and there is no reason to suppose that the inequities of the formal system will not be reproduced in the contemporary informal system (Abel 1982; Delgado 1985; Harrington 1982).

Barbara Yngvesson, in a recent review, addresses these issues by locating dispute resolution, or better, "disputing," in a structural and political context (Yngvesson 1988). In so doing, she draws the connections between the issues of power and autonomy discussed here in Chapter 1 and the sociology of organizations outlined in the next section. Yngvesson's major point is that "*disputes* can only be understood in the context of relationships that generate them and that *disputing* is intimately related to the negotiation of the social order" (Yngvesson:116; emphasis original). Yngvesson thus emphasizes that disputes arise out of the social, cultural, political, and economic forces that shape relationships and structure understandings. She, too, stresses the importance of ideology, language, the mobilization of bias, and the professionalization of knowledge: Structural frameworks empower or constrain. Power is central to the analysis. Unless these issues are addressed, the critics of alternative dispute resolution argue, the alternatives are only another form of social control over the powerless (Gallagher 1988).

Supporters of alternative dispute resolution claim that, at least under circumstances where the participants are talking to each other (the examples that Menkel-Meadow has in mind), there is also the opportunity for participants to connect with each other in more humanistic ways than in the formal system. Even though much of alternative dispute resolution is concerned with more appropriate solutions to concrete needs, as Menkel-Meadow argues, this is not inconsistent with the parties exploring more deeply into needs to gain greater understanding of oneself and others. Robert Bush, in reviewing much of the literature, argues that underlying many aspects of the alternative dispute resolution "movement" are competing visions of autonomy, personal transformation, corporatism, and community (Bush). We will return to this aspect of alternative dispute resolution when we consider the modern/postmodern philosophers in Chapter 6.

The Sociology of Organizations: From Weber to Garbage Cans

Thus far, in a variety of ways, we have discussed bureaucracy. The subject of this book is the relationship of the dependent person and large-scale public agencies. Chapter 1 discussed what happened to the legal rights project when confronted by bureaucracy. Regulatory reform starts with bureaucratic pathology and proposes restructuring; most alternative dispute resolution takes place within bureaucratic settings. Power in its various manifestations is mobilized through bureaucracy.

What is the nature of bureaucracy? Why has it colonized relationships? How can it be restructured? In a broad sense, the theoretical developments in law are following contemporary sociological theories of complex organizations, although with rare exceptions (Clune 1987; Frug 1984; Teubner 1983, 1986), there seems to be little awareness of these parallel developments.

Organizational theory has traveled from a Weberian rational perspective to natural, open, and political economy theories; along the way, there have also been Taylorism, human relations, decision-making, contingency, resource-dependency, and the garbage can model (Handler 1986). Although the course of this path has been described often and well, this section will summarize Yeheskel Hasenfeld's analysis and argument presented in *Human Service Organizations* (1983).

The rational perspective, with its emphasis on the specified goals that determine a formalized structure, is important as ideology. The concept of the rational bureaucracy is viewed as the norm, as the basic prerequisite of a modern, sophisticated, technological society. It is the standard by which we judge organizations (Ladd 1970). It is a conception of society that views implementation as neutral, rational, and efficient and has had much influence on traditional legal thought (Edelman 1971).

In a sense, contemporary organizational sociology is an industry devoted to disproving the Weberian model. Herbert Simon substituted the "satisficing," "administrative man" of bounded rationality for the "economic man." The natural systems school looked at organizations as collectivities, as social systems concerned primarily with survival. The loosely coupled, open system views organizations as shifting coalitions of special-interest groups, both internal and external to the organization, each pursuing its own goals and objectives, heavily influenced by the environment. The most radical view to date is the garbage can model of March and colleagues (1979), wherein problems, solutions, participants, and choice opportunities metaphorically are poured into a can; decisions result from the particular mixtures of these streams rather than from rational connections.

The political economy perspective, favored by Zald (1970), Hasenfeld, and others, attempts to combine the best features of these competing theories. The political economic theory focuses on the interaction between the political and economic forces that shape an organization's structure and processes; it is concerned with the processes through which power and social support (legitimacy) are acquired and distributed by the organization, operative goals are determined, and tasks are defined and controlled. Organizations are arenas in which various interest groups—both internal and external—compete with each other. The relative power of each group depends upon the importance of the resources it controls. Organizational processes are the exchange relations between the interest groups.

The major distinguishing features of post-Weberian perspectives can perhaps be summarized by two broad ideas. One concept holds that decisions, relations, activities, and transactions of organizational actors are only more or less, and probably mostly less, governed by formal rules and structures. The other concept emphasizes the importance of the environment: organizations are not closed systems, but are heavily influenced by their environmental context. The two ideals are interrelated since competing interest groups are both external and internal to the organization.

The mobilization of resources, both political and economic, is in part a function of the reciprocal relationships between the organization and its environment. Those who control the organization select those environmental resources that will enhance its position and reject those that challenge its position (Harrington and Merry). Internally, power depends on the importance of different units to the operative goals of the organization and on the resources (internal or external) that each unit can command.

The choice of technology is determined by the political and

economic processes that determine the distribution of power. The "product" of an organization strengthens the values of some groups at the expense of others. The environment is particularly important for human service organizations since they are so dependent on their environments for legitimation and money. They are influenced by the norms and characteristics of their local community—it is there that they acquire their legitimacy and their clients. The environment is thus both a set of resources and constraints.

Hasenfeld distinguishes between the *general* environment and the *task* environment. The general environment is the economic, demographic, cultural, political, legal, and technological context of the organization. The task environment refers to the set of organizations and groups with which the organization exchanges resources and services and establishes modes of interaction.

The general environment affects human service organizations by influencing the demand for human services; the characteristics of the clientele; the political, cultural, and value systems of the community; the legal structure of its operations; and the available technology. The organizational domain, in turn, is influenced by the task environment—its ability to mobilize the necessary resources through exchanges with external groups and organizations.

Thus, in order for an organization to be successful, it must obtain a fair amount of consensus about its activities from those who control the necessary resources. It must persuade other key actors in the environment that they, too, will benefit. The organization does this through negotiation, compromise, and exchange agreements.

There are at least two considerations to note in this model. First, it is dynamic: the organization seeks to contain uncertainty by adjusting to changes in the environment. And second, consensus does not have to take account of client interests as long as clients do not control access to key resources.

All organizations try to obtain some measure of control over their environments. If they have sufficient power, they can dictate the terms of the exchange. But this situation is rare, especially when human service organizations are involved. They can engage in competitive strategies—which usually means image building—but, in the most likely situation, they engage in cooperative strategies such as contracting, coalition building, or co-optation. Contracting is the most common strategy because human service organizations usually operate in networks where there are many organizations and few control substantial amounts of resources or services. Nevertheless, the strategies for reducing environmental uncertainty are usually only partially successful. Mostly, service networks are loosely coordinated and contain gaps, redundancies, and contradictions. There is no overall, rational system.

As discussed in Chapter 2, the human service organization seeks to change people; thus, its technology requires not only knowledge of the complexities of human behavior (no small task), but also that it be a *moral* system. By this, Hasenfeld means that clients are vested with moral and cultural values that define their status vis-à-vis the agency. Personal characteristics are not only not "objective"; they are also statements about social and moral status. The organization's pattern of intervention is crucially shaped by the staff's moral evaluation of the client. Moreover, as clients work their way through the system, they acquire additional social and moral attributes. The moral system incorporated in the technology encompasses, either explicitly or implicitly, a conception of human nature that provides the moral justification for the agency. The selection of the technology is the selection of a moral system that is then reinforced through the selection, processing, and evaluation of clients by the agency.

Another distinguishing feature of human service organization technology is its extensive reliance on face-to-face interactions between staff and clients. The interaction is critical; yet, the line staff—the "street-level bureaucrats"—are the most difficult to control because the visibility of their activity is limited. There may be legal or ethical restrictions on exposing the interaction. The practitioners are highly resistant to supervisory inquiry. They distrust the evaluation criteria and fear that the relationship with the client will be damaged. For the organization, administrative costs of this kind of supervision are high. Thus, the line staff not only generate most of the information for the organization, they also control access to that information.

On the other hand, the line staff are not entirely freewheeling. Often they are limited in their ability to control the context of where the work takes place. Case loads, working conditions, staff characteristics, and client characteristics all affect the context. Nonetheless, there is considerable discretion at the street level. The line staff utilize that discretion to promote their own interests, which may or may not coincide with the interest of the clients.

Who clients are and what roles they play are of major importance to the survival of the organization. It is through the clients that demands are registered. The characteristics of the clients affect the use of various technologies and the outputs of the organization. Hasenfeld rejects the commonly held view that the interests of the staff and the clients are compatible and that if there are client difficulties, it is due to the personal problems of the client. Rather, he sees a divergence of interests. Client interests derive from their individual attributes, whereas staff interests derive from the dynamics of the organization that shape the role of the staff. The outcome of the conflict—the ability of the staff to control the exchange relationship—depends on the power-dependency relationship, which, in many human service organizations, means that the staff retains considerable power. Staff members not only monopolize the services but also have many more clients than they can serve. The staff uses its power to select and deal with clients who will serve its interests, whether to confirm ideologies and status, control working conditions, or both.

Since the transformative abilities of the technologies are limited, the attributes of the clients who *enter* the system are very important in determining organizational success. Organizations establish patterns to attract and screen clients. Organizations that have the power to set their own admission criteria simply turn away unacceptable clients. Public agencies often lack this ability; they must develop informal mechanisms for dissuading certain clients and accepting others.

While clients often have limited options, there are constraints on organizational power. There are internal norms of fairness, equity, commitment to client needs, respect, and so forth, which Hasenfeld says should not be underestimated. There are also external norms such as legal rights and procedural due process, but, as noted in Chapter 2, the exercise of these restraints is problematic.

Connecting Themes

As stated previously, the topics in the preceding chapters and subsequent chapters in one way or another filter through bureaucracy. What, then, does organizational sociology tell us about developments in law, regulation, and alternative dispute resolution? How does organizational sociology relate to the themes of jurisprudence outlined in the next chapter?

At a descriptive level, traditional legal thought envisioned Weberian rationality. While not totally unsophisticated, law tended to view implementation of positive legal norms in rational, neutral, bureaucratic terms. At times there would be slippage and disobedience, but compliance with norms was considered to be the norm. In the present era, this conception of formalism has been seriously questioned. Many see rules as dysfunctional for the regulatory task. All see widespread discretion and bargaining. Organizational sociology has long since abandoned the Weberian model. It sees bargaining, flexibility, exchange, and discretion as the norm. As we shall see in the next chapter, there is a close affinity between March's garbage cans and critical legal studies.

Contemporary organizational sociology parallels the Continental systems analysis of Niklas Luhmann and Gunther Teubner (Chapter 4). The open-system, political economy model seems to be another way of describing Luhmann's functionally differentiated society. Teubner's "structured coupling" or reflexivity restates the sociological description of organizations attempting to manage environmental uncertainty through exchange relationships. A key point in both strands of thought, and a sharp contrast to the Weberian model, involves causality in implementation. Traditional implementation analysis as well as conventional legal policy analysis assume a more or less linear cause-and-effect relationship between policy initiatives and behavior. The Weberian ideology of the rational bureaucracy is implicit. Contemporary implementation and systems analysis, organizational sociology, and Continental reflexive law challenge this assumption. Implementation is not a matter of linear cause and effect. When implementation occurs—never a certainty—it does so primarily through bargaining, negotiation, compromise, and other forms of exchange relationships among the competing organizations (Handler and Zatz 1982).

Sociologists, by temperament, eschew normative concerns and, in most of the standard works, it is difficult to find such concerns explicitly discussed. However, there is a growing body of literature that looks favorably on the possibilities of discretion, the freedom of action, revealed by contemporary analysis. As will be discussed in the next chapter, Luhmann and Teubner view reflexivity as the most promising mechanism of social integration. Some social scientists think that contemporary implementation analysis will lead to more intelligent social planning (Elmore 1980; Handler and Zatz 1982). And, of course, those who have argued against command-and-control regulation and in favor of more cooperative styles think that discretion can be used to fashion more appropriate forms of regulation, better substantive justice, and better substantive procedural decisions among people.

In Hasenfeld's discussion of client-staff interactions, normative concerns are explicit. The issue of power cries out for normative judgments, and Hasenfeld, in his opening statement, observes that the individual's loss of power vis-à-vis human service organizations is one of the fundamental characteristics of the welfare state. His description of the consequences of the moral typification process of clients in human service organizations captures the manifestations of power described by Lukes, Gaventa, and Yngvesson and, as discussed in the next chapter, elucidates Habermas's argument that the social welfare state has redefined human relations and destroyed communicative action in the life-world.

Hasenfeld argues that the greater the uncertainty about the consequences of agency intervention, the greater the need for persuasion rather than coercion. He urges trust, cooperative relations between staff and clients, flexibility tolerance, and mutual commitments (Hasenfeld 1983:128). Hasenfeld thinks that interventions can only be successful when there is mutual trust. These ideas are quite similar to those expressed by Hawkins, Menkel-Meadow, and others who urge a cooperative, problem-solving style for regulation. The themes of trust and cooperation have been adopted by radical feminists and modern/postmodern ethical philosophers, as discussed in Chapters 4 and 5.

Chapter 4
Trends in Jurisprudence

Two major, complementary themes stand out in the developments just described: first, that many important social conflicts cannot be solved through the application of legal rules in the classical liberal legal mode; and second, that space has to be created within structural (legal) frameworks to allow for the more flexible, creative resolution of conflicts. Both of these ideas have roots in three contemporary jurisprudential themes: the attack on liberal legalism begins with legal realism and its contemporary heir, critical legal studies; the second is feminist jurisprudence; and the third is reflexive law developed by Continental theorists.

Legal Realism and Critical Legal Studies

Legal realism was a complex movement. Two components of the movement are important for our purposes. First, it successfully attacked the formalist "fantasy" that there is a universal scheme of neutral, general rules that decide cases; instead, it postulated that law is "animated by social purposes and policies" (Gordon 1984). Second, legal realism saw that law is indeterminate. By indeterminacy, legal realists meant that legal rules did not necessarily decide cases. Legal rules themselves were often vague; in addition, there were always clusters of rules that could be applied to a single case. Thus, in any given situation, the judge could extract rules or meanings of particular rules at will. Because the law did not dictate these choices, the law did not determine the outcome (Altman 1986).

What, then, did determine the outcome? According to legal realism, underlying political values. Indeed, according to Andrew

Altman, the "breakdown of any sharp distinction between law (adjudication) and politics... is the master theme of legal realism" (Altman:207, n. 4). Law is policy; law is politics. Mark Tushnet draws the connection between this aspect of realism and the progressive intellectual traditions of the 1920s and 1930s (Tushnet 1986). Just as the legal realists attacked formalist theories of abstract, neutral law, the progressive thinkers attacked the historical, functional ideas of unfolding progress within a generally liberal framework. Instead, the progressives saw the interplay of competing interest groups. In both the legislatures and the courts, power politics was the reality. This aspect of legal realism, in the argot of today, consisted of demystification. The mythic ideology of value-free, neutral law was destroyed.

The realists' ideology also had a constructive aspect. Legal policymakers, in rejecting deduction and intuition from abstract legal rules, were to utilize explicit, systematic policy analysis. They were to identify the relevant interests, analyze effects of alternative courses of action (including the legal system), and balance the interests at stake using social science techniques. The results, however, were far from being the arbitrary, ad hoc outcome of the temporary alignment of naked forces. Rather, the realists believed that important, abstract ethical and social ideals underlay legal and policy choices—for example, human freedom and material well-being. While there might be disagreement as to how these basic values would be advanced or whether competing values ought also to be considered, policy would ultimately be grounded on these broadly shared understandings. Tushnet argues that the constructive program of the legal realists is the dominant framework for most legal thought today (Tushnet).

Critical legal studies (CLS) accepts the critical part of legal realism but, using the same techniques, attacks the constructive part—the policy analysis, the balancing, and the idea that there are shared social values that can resolve disputes. Social values, like legal rules, are so abstract that they can be used to justify any decision. Law may be infused with ethical ideals and values, but these values are competing and irreconcilable. Rather than seeking out some underlying, agreed-upon shared value, the decisionmaker must still pick and choose. More important, these values are not abstract and timeless; rather, they are structured by contemporary society; rather than coherent ethical theories, they are the temporary outcome of ideological power struggles and compromises (Altman). While at any given time practices may be settled, it is not possible to arrive at settled, principled justifications of those practices (Kelman 1987).

In this important respect, critical legal studies goes much further than legal realism. According to Tushnet, the dominant CLS strain insists that no general social-theoretical explanations are available. CLS believes that our lives are structured by the institutions that we create and sustain, and that they have no meaning outside of those institutions and processes (see also Peller 1987). As soon as a general theory or explanation is offered, the task is to "decenter" the explanation by rearranging the terms and categories to show that an alternative explanation is just as plausible. Thus far, the "decentering project" has no termination; the politics of decentering are to disrupt whatever understandings happen to become settled, criticize every existing order (Tushnet), and shatter the "congealed forms of life by showing that they have no particular integrity" (Gordon). Since the legal system is deeply implicated in structuring the present order, it is essentially illegitimate (Altman; Kelman).

Critical legal studies is fundamentally concerned with power and community. In contrast to liberals who equate the separateness of the individual with autonomy and freedom, CLS sees liberal individualism as alienation and loneliness. They believe that true subjective desires are attachment, connection with others, and that it is through the recognition of others that one becomes enlivened and empowered (Gabel 1989; R. West 1988). The CLS passion is to attack illegitimate hierarchy, domination, and oppression, and to democratize all social forms. It attacks the legal realists' constructive program on the grounds that those who do the balancing belong to elites and do not represent the powerless in society; moreover, they have been socialized into particular sets of beliefs that preserve their positions of power and privilege. Truth claims play powerful political roles in constructing our social relations; they serve to justify the powerful and to make the weak feel that they are at fault and inadequate (Foucault 1980 and 1986; Peller). An important example of this is the language of social gender roles where power is not the result of some "objective, natural reality" but rather "a construct with a particular history and place" (Peller:95). Law is a discourse that transforms power into "knowledge" through its various rules, codes, and conventions (Norris 1988). The politics of deconstruction is to expose the reproduction of illegitimate authority and power in our everyday language and methodologies (Peller). The positive project of deconstruction is to empower those who are oppressed. It is through deconstruction that the human personality will be emancipated and allowed to flourish (Unger 1975).

The full implications of the CLS attack on formalism are manifest in its controversial critique of civil rights, those laws specifically designed to empower dependent people. It asserts that the regime of civil rights has not only resulted in false promises—that is, civil rights, in fact, have not been realized—but that legal rights have actually served to *disempower,* to make worse, the lives of those whom they were designed to protect (Gabel and Kennedy 1984). Laws granting *formal* equality have legitimized underlying political, economic, and social inequalities. The existence of civil rights laws on the books has persuaded the majority that equality has now been accorded and that existing inequalities are the fault of the victim (Pettigrew). Thus, inequalities have been legalized (Tushnet; Freeman 1988; Bumiller) and the regime of rights has drawn attention away from the needs of victims (Tushnet). The effect, says Peter Gabel, is that rights are "integrated within an ideological framework that has as its ultimate aim the maintenance of collective passivity" (Gabel and Kennedy:36; see also Gordon 1984; Tushnet 1986). In addition, when legal rights are used, they destroy the quality of participation: they impose formality on relations and barriers to communication; they create zones of privacy and alienation rather than bonds of mutual responsibility (Freeman; Gabel; Unger). These arguments are similar to the ones that were raised against the liberal legal approach of "The New Property"; formal equality, the appearance of neutrality, in fact, results in alienation and legal domination (Gabel; Lempert 1980–81; R. West).

The CLS critique of rights has been strongly criticized, especially by blacks and feminists. Patricia Williams points out that the informal system, the system of no rights made blacks vulnerable to white assaults. This was true not only during slavery, but also up until the present-day enactment and enforcement of civil rights law, which began a scant two decades ago. Blacks, she argues, are not so naive as to believe in the complete efficacy of rights. Yet, it was legal rights that began to give them some measure of autonomy and dignity. In direct opposition to CLS, Williams argues that rights and the barriers that are erected by formalism empower blacks, and that blacks need to protect themselves from white intrusions. In the black experience, "the concept of rights, both positive and negative is the marker of our civilization, our participatoriness, our relation to others" (Williams 1987: 431). Without rights, blacks were objects to be used by those holding the rights (Delgado 1987). In Kimberlé Crenshaw's words, blacks were brought into the American political imagination once they gained rights; she argues that it is the "failure of the Critics [CLS] to contextualize the critique of rights [that is, consider rights in the context of American racism] which leads to an inability to appreciate the transformative significance of the civil rights movement which mobilized Black Americans and generated new demands" (Crenshaw 1988; C. West 1988).

What these black writers are saying is that before there can be participation, community, or attachment, there has to be autonomy. Formalism, legal rights, as exemplified in the civil rights struggle, helped blacks in their struggle for autonomy. They had to conceive of themselves as rights-bearing citizens in order to generate their demands for participation in American society (Crenshaw). In this important sense, civil rights were constitutive of the black struggle (Brigham 1987). CLS argues that autonomy created through the ideology of legal rights prevents participation; that the ideology of rights is incompatible with solidarity (Gabel). While acknowledging the limitations of legal rights (Bell 1987), minority scholars argue that, in their experiences, civil rights not only empowered minorities, but, in sharp contrast to the CLS position, also created solidarity (Dalton 1987; Delgado 1987; Crenshaw; Matsuda 1987; Williams). These themes are picked up by Martha Minow, who argues that rights and rights consciousness can enhance participation; rights are claims on behalf of people that they are members of the community, that they are to be listened to and respected (Minow 1987; Cornell 1985).

Feminist Jurisprudence

There are, by now, a wide range of feminist theories and jurisprudence (Littleton 1989); all of them, however, are fundamentally concerned with power and view the legal system as deeply implicated in the oppression of women in contemporary society. Much of feminist jurisprudence comprises women's rights law. Its objective is to secure those rights for women that men enjoy under contemporary legal arrangements; as such, it fits within conventional American liberal legal reform. Women have long fought for equal rights in property, contracts, family law, and, of course, voting. The liberal legal reform struggles today continue in important areas of employment, access, crime, and family law. In many aspects of life, the feminist struggle is very similar to the struggles of persons of color. While many formal legal barriers have been struck down, major, serious inequalities remain.

More radical or communitarian feminists either oppose or express ambivalence about the liberal legal feminist project. They acknowledge the importance of the historical contributions, and recognize that today major law reform has to be achieved in those situations where the legal system is particularly oppressive. Nonetheless, communitarian feminists argue that the liberal legal approach has serious limitations. In the tradition of the legal realists and critical legal studies, these feminists believe that rights analysis is indeterminate; in any given situation, it cannot decide specific cases—when differences in treatment will be justified or not (Olsen 1984)—and that traditional equality law ultimately proves to be inadequate in the face of significant differences (Frug 1987).

The feminist communitarian critique, however, goes deeper. Its point of view is that the liberal legal equality doctrine is fundamentally inconsistent with feminism. The liberal legal approach implicitly accepts a male view of the world, it devalues the most fundamental social characteristics of women, and its concern with the primacy of abstract, neutral rules is ultimately limited and incapable of seriously addressing the core issues of domination (Ferguson 1984; Littleton; Scales 1986; R. West). The women's rights approach seeks to assimilate women into the male standard. Although this does not rule out affirmative action or special treatment to overcome specific instances of socialization or prejudice, the ultimate aim is assimilation (Frug 1987). Feminists who reject the assimilationist position take different positions. Some think that law is part of male domination; it is ideologically oppressive to women; it is fundamentally patriarchal. By using law one accepts its basic paradigm, reinforces patriarchy, and gives tacit approval to the basic social order. Others are willing to use law to relieve specific instances of oppression.

Robin West explains the radical and communitarian feminist positions by contrasting them with liberal legalism and critical legal studies. She draws a distinction between the "separation thesis" and the "connection thesis." The male theories—liberal legalism and CLS—view people as materially separate from each other and the natural world. In classical liberal terms, the individual is "presocial." The liberal view, which is the dominant view, celebrates separation. It is the source of freedom. Freedom from the other means freedom to develop one's own life plans. The fear of the liberal is that others will not respect his freedom and will impose their goals. Since all people are equally free, the goal of government is to respect and maintain this individual freedom and not allow invasion by others. Government, indeed, society, is neutral as to the good life (R. West).

Critical legal studies, according to West, also views the individual as separate, but argues that the individual does not flourish under the liberal conception, but subjectively experiences loneliness and alienation, and longs for community. It is through connection with others that individuals become empowered. Whereas liberals fear invasion, CLS thinks that individuals most fear isolation.

West maintains that feminist theory also divides along a similar axis. "Cultural" feminists embrace the connection thesis, which—in contrast to the liberal theory of individuals as "presocial"—holds that women are epistemologically and morally connected to other life from the very beginning. Because women rear children, they are fundamentally connected, not separated, from others; they have different ways of experiencing life than men. Women value intimacy and develop a capacity for nurturance and an ethic of care for the other. They dread separation; instead, women construct social relations. Morality is not judged in terms of the liberal ideal of maintaining rights in the face of other individuals; rather, its standard is responsibility to others. Cultural feminists have redefined women's differences so that what was seen as weakness is now perceived as strength. "[I]ntimacy is not just something women *do,* it is something human beings *ought* to do. Intimacy is a source of value, not a private hobby. It is morality, not habit" (R. West:18).

Radical feminists agree with the culturalists about the caring characteristics of women, but hold to an opposite morality. They view connection with the other as invasive and as a threat to autonomy. They argue that although officially women may celebrate connection, subjectively they long for deliverance and independence. Catharine MacKinnon, for example, argues that the values of caring and connection have been imposed on women by men, and that women work toward these values because these are the traits for which men value women (MacKinnon 1987). Whereas cultural feminists believe that the good life is relational, contextual, affective, and involves caring for the weak and dependent, the radical feminists view connection as the source of women's subordination and debasement. Whereas cultural feminists celebrate pregnancy as the source of morality, the radical feminists view intercourse and pregnancy as an invasion, a breach of the boundary between self and others. Intimacy is invasive and oppressive (R. West).

The dominant male ideology (liberal) rejects the male who seeks others; the dominant female ideology rejects the woman who seeks separation. The deviant male ideology (CLS) seeks connection; the deviant female ideology seeks separation. Nevertheless, argues West, there is a difference between the connectedness theories of CLS and the cultural feminists. Men must learn how to love; they have to overcome separation through social construction. Women naturally love; separation is socially constructed. Thus, radical feminists use the ideology and tools of liberal legalism. They seek to extend rights to create autonomy for women (R. West).

West argues that both liberal theory and critical theory are "masculine jurisprudence." By this she means that men are both the authors and the beneficiaries of the law; and women's lives are simply not taken as seriously as are men's. To create a feminist jurisprudence, patriarchy must be abolished. The first project, then, of a feminist jurisprudence is to expose and critique the patriarchy that is behind ungendered law and theory. Second, there must be "reconstructive jurisprudence," one that values intimacy not only for women, but for the entire community. Thus far, feminist rights law has won many reform victories but has done so by analogizing to male harms. Now it is time to rearticulate these new rights in terms of women's distinctive existential and material experiences. It must recognize the importance of love, which is currently lacking in public life and not rewarded in private life (R. West).

Communitarian feminists differ from the liberal legal approach on the issues of power and participation. According to Kathy Ferguson, communitarian feminists conflate the issues of power and the quality of participation. This occurs because the personality is not taken as given, as prior to social relations (as in the liberal position), but rather is constituted through the very processes of social interaction. The feminist conception of social interaction enhances autonomy (empowerment) and community simultaneously. The goal of communitarian feminism is to value and nurture the care-based qualities of women as distinguished from the rights-based approach of men. Communitarian feminists are interested in the quality of interpersonal relations, in social bonds. They believe that social bonds are both constitutive and transformative; that the human personality is created through the process of interacting with others.

Communitarian feminists do not deny the value of individualism, but they see a dialectic. They see individualism as flourishing only within relationships, not in isolation. Communities can foster both individuality and connectedness because caring for others entails caring for their freedom. A community based on the caretaking qualities of feminism would recognize the "dialectical need for connectedness within freedom and for diversity within solidarity" (Ferguson:196).[8]

Men, in contrast, are interested in rights. They seek justice through the application of abstract, uniformly applied rules. Legal rights and rules draw boundaries between self and others. Men resolve disputes in terms of who is right according to rules; women explore needs and see if both sides can be satisfied.

Classic, liberal legal reform on behalf of women accepts the male view. Its agenda is to seek entry, not to change the rules of the game. Communitarian feminists are not content to gain entry into the male world only to become like men. This point is brought out in Kathy Ferguson's analysis of feminism and bureaucracy. She argues that the power structures generated by bureaucratic capitalist society are the primary source of oppression of both men and women and that the system of bureaucratic domination and subordination reflects the power relations between men and women in the society

---

8. For a more cautionary view of the relationship between community and feminist aspirations, see Friedman (1989) and Young (1986), discussed in Chapter 5.

at large. Capitalist bureaucracies isolate individuals, depersonalize social relations, mask domination under the guise of efficiency, destroy interpersonal connections and intimacy, and fragment lives. Such relations are fundamentally dehumanizing, since Ferguson believes that the human self is only created by the processes of interacting with others. Isolation also has political consequences in that it limits the shared experiences necessary to redefine alternatives (Ferguson).

How does bureaucracy specifically affect women? Ferguson argues that there are two dimensions to women's experiences: There is the positive, creative dimension—caretaking, responding to the needs of others, empathy, nurturance, and cooperation, where people are interrelated rather than opposed to each other. In this dimension—she calls this "femaleness"—women assume responsibility for others; judgments are made in context rather than in abstraction; the focus is more on process rather than outcome. The other dimension—"feminization"—involves the characteristics of women as victims of male domination. Femaleness makes women vulnerable. The need for others implicitly raises the possibility of loss and encourages the avoidance of risk and conflict. Vulnerability leads to exploitation and victimization. Partly as a result of women's caretaking, men are able to subordinate women in both public and private life.

Bureaucracy rewards the "male" characteristics (analytic, independent, rational, competitive, instrumental) and devalues "female" characteristics (supportive, nonassertive, dependent, expressive). As bureaucracy rewards dominating characteristics, it "feminizes" subordinates. The needs to please, avoid risk and confrontation, conform, and be dependent are the "avenues by which the powerless make the best of a bad situation" (Ferguson:98); Ferguson calls this "impression management." Women learn the subordinate role to protect themselves in the bureaucratic structure, but by becoming feminized they perpetuate their own subordination. It is bureaucratic capitalism that distorts the caring characteristics of women. Patriarchal power has turned caring into the service of male supremacy; women develop impression management in order to survive.

Ferguson's vision is of a society in which the female characteristics of caring, nurturing, and relating to others through the process of collective lives can flourish. She thinks that it is not possible to create such a society within bureaucracies. The feminist vision is a *"deliberately anti-bureaucratic vision"* (Ferguson:190; emphasis original). Liberalism only extends bureaucratic capitalism; women who are lucky enough to gain access will become like men. The caretaking qualities of women cannot flourish in hierarchy. Instead, public life must be restructured to allow for the intimacy of human relations in personal, face-to-face encounters.

In sum, communitarian feminist jurisprudence differs from critical legal studies insofar as it is explicitly animated, root and branch, by a concrete view of human relations and has an active, constructive political agenda. The current legal order is illegitimate; but a feminist legal order (encompassing men who become feminist) would be legitimate. However, the legal order envisaged by communitarian feminists would not resemble the current legal order even if the power of the sexes were reversed. Human relations would not be governed by abstract, universal rules pretending to be objective and neutral. In Ferguson's view, this would only change women into men. To liberate, maintain, and develop the nurturing and caretaking qualities of women, the legal system must be decentralized and contextualized; it must deal with concrete situations; and it must facilitate, not destroy, the communitarian feminist vision of human interaction.

Continental Theories of Reflexive Law

The kind of legal order required for human interaction is the subject of the final topic in the area of jurisprudence. In the jurisprudential discussion thus far, there has been convergence on the need for a decentralized legal system that provides arenas for cooperation, flexibility, contextualization—the communitarian feminist vision of human interaction. The present legal order, however, produced the centralized, hierarchical legal-bureaucratic regime. In the discussion of regulatory unreasonableness in the previous chapter some of these issues were introduced. Continental jurisprudence, or reflexive law, and the work of Jürgen Habermas provide a more systematic or theoretical account of the reasons for the legal-bureaucratic regime, and offer an analysis of how this trend should be reversed.

The rise of the contemporary social welfare state imposed distinct changes in the character and functions of the legal system. As conceptualized by Max Weber, law evolved from formal rationality, or autonomous law, to substantive rationality. Autonomous law is conceptually abstract, precise, and procedural; its rules of interpretation strive for uniformity and continuity. Autonomous law seeks to resolve social conflicts without regard to ethical, political, economic, or social consequences. It was supposed to be substantively neutral. As such, it fit the needs of the rising bourgeoisie by providing for the maximum amount of market freedom and certainty (Teubner 1983).

Substantive elements began to enter the legal system. Beginning at least by the end of the nineteenth century, the state began to regulate abuses or imperfections of the market and law became increasingly particularistic. Over time, legislative and judicial intervention in the content of commercial arrangements increased, and law began to reflect explicit normative considerations (Teubner 1983). In this century, with the rise in regulation, there has been a vast increase in the use of law to accomplish specific substantive goals in concrete situations. Law has changed from formal rationality to substantive rationality.

Gunther Teubner, building on the work of Niklas Luhmann and Jürgen Habermas, argues that this change to substantive or purposive law is part of the crisis of the regulatory state. The crisis of law in the modern state can be variously defined as overregulation, lack of effectiveness, or a failure of implementation. Since law now serves as one of the major instruments of the welfare state, enormous demands have been placed upon it. To be able to discharge effectively its burden of directly regulating vast and diverse social areas, law must incorporate massive new bodies of social, economic, and scientific knowledge into the legal system. So far, argues Teubner, law has not been able to meet these demands (Teubner 1983).

There are large costs entailed in trying to make law more instrumentally effective. One line of criticism comes from the theory of Habermas. In the modern democratic welfare state, the increasingly complex and internally dense economy, supported by the state, extends its formal domains into other subsystems or life-worlds such as the family, schools, and other relationships heretofore not governed by law. Through the interchange of subsystems, there is a growth of a whole complex of relationships that is bureaucratically coordinated (Habermas 1987). The symbolic reproductions of lifeworlds are converted through the medium of money and state bureaucratic power. Habermas calls this the "colonization of the lifeworld." "The imperatives of autonomous subsystems make their way into the lifeworld from the outside—like colonial masters coming into a tribal society—and force a process of assimilation upon it" (Habermas 1987:355). The major example that he uses is "juridification"—the tendency to increase the use of formal or positive law in areas that were previously regulated only informally.

Examples of juridification in the economy include the regulation of working hours, the freedom of unions to organize, and the provision of social security, which involve relationships previously exercised by the private owners of the means of production. The extension of the economy and the state has had ambivalent results. The beneficient effects of the modern welfare state have cushioned the harshness of wage labor, but the harmful effects of juridification, argues Habermas, endanger the freedom of the beneficiaries.

Habermas distinguishes between law as "medium" and law as "institution" (Habermas 1986). Using social welfare policy for illustration, he argues that while the accomplishments of law as medium may be undeniable, it also significantly alters, if not destroys, important human relationships. This occurs because the structure of legal systems establishes *individual* entitlements under *specific* general legal conditions. Bureaucratic implementation furthers the process of abstraction and redefinition. The administrator has to apply general legal conditions to the concrete social problem. The claimant and family are "embedded in the context of a life-history and a concrete way of life," but are redefined legally and handled administratively, and subjected to "violent abstraction" in order to meet the bureaucratic demands of a large, centralized, distant, and computerized organization.

An example that Habermas uses involves the modern welfare state's practice of meeting the problems caused by retirement or job loss with cash payments. Providing cash benefits in the event of illness or old age redefines the self-image of the beneficiary and his or her family relations. State social security pensions and public assistance also profoundly affect the role of community in providing charity. Thus, the specification of the legal conditions under which public compensation will be given inevitably exerts pressure to redefine everyday situations (Habermas 1987).

Habermas argues that money is often inadequate in view of the full dimensions of the loss; thus, social services are needed. The therapeutic interventions, in turn, for the most part increase client dependency. The irony, according to Habermas, is that because core areas of the life-world have become bureaucratized and monetized, the welfare state has to spread a network of agency-client relationships over what were formerly private life spheres. But the contradictions of welfare state interventions are only reproduced at a higher level—the client of the "therapeutocracy" becomes even more dependent on the state expert who is supposed to promote independence and self-reliance (Habermas 1987). Habermas observes that "while the welfare state guarantees are intended to serve the goal of social integration, they nevertheless promote the disintegration of life relations" (Habermas 1986:213). The more the welfare state tries to cushion the social effects of the economy on these private spheres of life, the more there are likely to be the pathological side effects of juridification. Legalized interventions, by their very structure, separate and disintegrate consensual relations.

The family and schools are two other examples that display the same ambivalence as social security law. The rights of children, wives, pupils, teachers, and parents have all been enacted to establish constitutional principles. But these rights, which require a high degree of specification of conditions, exceptions, and consequences, open up these spheres to bureaucratic and judicial intervention. Previously, socialization—moral in the family, pedagogical in the schools—took place through communicative action. Legalization supplants this communicative context with legal norms: relations become formalized; family members, pupils, teachers, and parents now encounter each other as legal subjects. The relationships are converted to the medium of law, but the abstractness of law applies without regard to the specific needs and interests of the persons involved. The same result has occurred with child custody laws.

Although the intervention of the state has been justified on the grounds of the need to counter domination within the family, a new form of dependency has taken its place; the family is now subordinate to the court and the youth-welfare office—the parties are now *subjects* of the proceedings rather than *participants* (Habermas 1987: 369). Juridification of these relationships occurs because public welfare policy uses law as a medium to regulate interpersonal relations. On a broad front, Habermas sees the dominating grip of modern capitalism and legalization, the internal colonization by the legal-bureaucratic systems.

Habermas does not want to abandon the gains of the modern social welfare system. His concern is with the bureaucratic means of implementing these goals. Habermas calls for law to operate as an "institution" rather than as a steering medium. By this he means that legal institutions should function as "external constitutions" in order to "protect areas of life that are functionally dependent on social integration through values, norms, and consensus formation, to preserve them from falling prey to the systemic imperatives of economic and administrative subsystems growing with dynamics of their own, and to defend them from becoming converted over, through the steering mechanisms of the law, to a principle of socialization that is, for them, dysfunctional" (Habermas 1987:364). Law should establish procedures for settling conflicts that facilitate communicative action. In schools, for example, the framework of the constitution should provide for decision-making procedures oriented toward reaching consensus and "treat those involved in the process as having the capacity to represent their own interests and to regulate their affairs themselves" (Habermas 1986:220). The relation of clients to public service agencies should be reconstituted in a "participatory mode" (Habermas 1987:394).

Niklas Luhmann, from the perspective of system theory, also argues against the continued expansion of substantive rationality in law. Modern society is a functionally differentiated social system, and the legal system is one of its functional subsystems. Each subsystem is constituted in terms of its functions. Given functional differentiation, each subsystem has to have a certain measure of autonomy because no other subsystem can do that function (Luhmann 1988).

The functional subsystems are "self-referential." By this, Luhmann means that they presuppose and reproduce themselves. Luhmann draws on the analogy of "autopoiesis," whose central tenet is that a system produces and reproduces its own elements and thereby achieves closure (Luhmann 1988). Like other systems, the legal system is an information-processing system. Normatively, the system refers to its own self-reproduction; cognitively, it adapts to environmental demands. These demands are selectively filtered by the legal system according to the logic of its own norms. Thus, the legal system is both open and closed in that legal change reflects its own internal dynamic, which both is affected by the environment and, in turn, influences the environment (Luhmann 1988; Teubner 1988a).

According to Luhmann, the "crisis" of the modern regulatory state arises from the inability of the legal system to adjust the complexities of a functionally differentiated society composed of semi-autonomous subsystems. What has happened is an enormous overproduction of positive law (substantive rationality) which inappropriately interferes with other subsystems and at the same time also threatens the integrity of the legal system. Law faces a massive information problem. Because legal doctrine is still bound to classical models of enforcing rules through adjudication, it lacks the capacity to compare the consequences of different solutions to problems in order to facilitate social planning among the various specialized subsystems. In short, law has not yet developed the capacity to "learn" (Teubner 1983). Rather than trying to enforce uniform norms (substantive rationality) across the specialized subsystems, societal integration must be decentralized to allow for the specific rationality of the functionally differentiated subsystems.

How, then, is integration to be achieved? The different subsystems must be mutually supportive; while pursuing their own functions, they have to be compatible with the functions of other subsystems in their environment. *Reflexion* is the mechanism by which each subsystem imposes internal restrictions on itself, thus allowing for integration with other subsystems (Teubner 1983).

Gunther Teubner develops the concept of "reflexive law" in answer to the question, How can the legal system cope with an overly complex environment? (Teubner 1983, 1984, 1986). The key, according to Teubner, is self-regulation. As previously stated, when law is the steering medium of the welfare state, it is either ineffective (symbolic only) or it destroys the traditional patterns of social life. This occurs because regulatory law is incompatible with the internal logic of the subsystems that it tries to regulate. Law must be relieved of the burden of direct regulation and allow for self-regulation (Teubner 1986). The destructive effects of colonization are mutual; interacting subsystems lose their differential functions. In the modern welfare state, according to Luhmann, the legal system itself is in danger. Its code is threatened when legal decisions are made in terms of "beneficial and harmful rather than the difference between legal and illegal." Through "social engineering" doctrines, "one may reach the point where the anti-trust courts can no longer be distinguished from the anti-trust agency, or youth courts from the youth welfare office itself" (Luhmann 1988:347; Nelkin 1988).

Teubner argues that law could accomplish integrative functions if the legal system were to become "reflexive." To be successfully integrative, law must recognize and seek to cope with the self-referential structures of regulated areas. The regulated subsystems also consist of elements engaged in reproductive interaction. These structures are, of course, influenced by regulation, but only within the limits of their own autopoietic adaptation. Unless there is "structural coupling" (appropriate integration between subsystems), there will be three paths to regulatory failure: Law will produce no change at all; it will be symbolic only. There will be "over-legalization" (Habermas's colonization), and traditional patterns of social life will be destroyed. Or law will become "over-socialized"; that is, law will be "captured" by the regulated subsystem (Luhmann's concern). The common failure, according to Teubner, is that regulatory law turns out to be ineffective; it overreaches the inherent limitations of the regulatory process because it fails to deal with the self-referentiality of the regulated subsystems. The basic problem is lack of knowledge: the legal system cannot acquire sufficient information about other self-referential systems.

How, then, is reflexive law to regulate? Teubner uses an approach similar to Habermas's concept of law as institution. By restricting law to its external constitutional role, it can facilitate consensus-oriented procedures as a method of regulation. Reflexive law tries to create freedom within limited autonomous areas. In school law, the external constitution would seek to limit pressures from the state, the administration, and the economy to allow teachers, parents, and pupils to reflect on the basic orientation of education (Teubner 1986). The redesign of decision-making procedures is the core element of reflexive law. A favorite example of Teubner, as well as of Habermas, is collective bargaining, where law was a major mechanism for changing power inside the organization. At the same time, law did not act as the steering medium for the substantive terms of the employment contract.

Whereas regulatory law fails because it lacks the requisite knowledge to allow it to intervene effectively in the regulated subsystems, the knowledge needed for reflexive law is considerably less. Reflexive law is not engaged in comprehensive planning; rather, it is procedural regulation and concentrates on the relations between systems. According to Teubner, this drastically reduces the cognitive requirements on the legal system.

The reflexive law and jurisprudence of Habermas seem to imply a significant normative democratic agenda. As stated, one of the favorite examples of Teubner and Habermas is collective bargaining. Other terms, such as "consensus-oriented procedures," participatory mechanisms in various social subsystems, pragmatic dialogue models, and the "democratization of social subsystems," imply democratic participation. Reflexive law as external constitution is a precondition for Habermas's ideal speech situation, where there are "no social constraints, no power relations, to distort the exchange of information and the formation of concensus" (Hoy 1985:62). Teubner, however, in his latest statement, seeks to strip all normative elements from reflexive law: "Power equalization is not the primary aspect of reflexive law. It is only important if certain social goals are expected to be achieved through symmetrical power relations" (Teubner 1986). Other models of society—for example, growth—might require an increase in the power of certain members or leaders in organizations. Reflexive law is designed to be responsive to human needs, and that may not mean the neutralization of power (Teubner 1986). David Nelkin goes further: the attempt to use law to compensate for maldistributions of power would politicize law and destroy its legitimacy. Rather, the function of reflexive or autopoietic law is to absorb and depoliticize problems which are not solved in the political process (Nelkin).

This last point—the importance of functional differentiation and reflexivity in preserving the internal integrity of societal subsystems—is addressed in an article by Christine Harrington which implicitly draws together the themes of Continental reflexive law and the arguments against command-and-control regulation developed in Chapter 3 (Harrington 1988).

Harrington's article is particularly illuminating because, in contrast to the literature thus far discussed, she is critical of deregulation and informalism and the creation of private spheres of action. Her particular concern is the current move toward "negotiation"—the process by which administrative rules are developed through the negotiation of interested parties rather than by the more formal administrative procedures. As seen in Chapter 3, this process was the program called for by those who wanted to roll back command-and-control regulation and extend cooperative-style regulation above the field level into policy-making. The impetus for negotiated rule-making, Harrington tells us, is the concern over the breakdown of administrative regulation and, as with alternative dispute resolution in civil and criminal justice, an antipathy to the adversarial approach. On a more abstract level, these concerns bridge the jurisdictional themes of the Continental theorists and the communitarian feminists.

Harrington uses as her example of regulatory negotiation the proposals of the Administrative Conference of the United States. The conference recommends that either the agency or a member of the regulated community initiate the regulatory process by designating an outside private facilitator or mediator to help reach agreements. Among the many claimed advantages of such a system is the theory that the participation by the parties would be more direct and of a higher quality. Harrington notes that the emphasis today is no longer on the fact of participation (formal due process) but on the *form* of participation. The agency would be one of the participants. The legitimacy of the process would be based on group consensus rather than public procedures.

Harrington argues that although the rhetoric of regulatory negotiation or deregulation is cast in terms of participant communication, its ideology is an old image of the market. By this she means that the state is to withdraw from its regulatory role so that the self-balancing market system may reassert itself:

> The vision of state-market relations is one in which self-balancing incentives operate to express and accommodate conflict and overcome private and public coercion.... The state becomes one of the interested parties in regulatory negotiation because it is seen as being too biased to police effectively the market and achieve high levels of voluntary compliance. (Harrington 1988:307)

Traditional regulation is concerned with agency discretion and unwarranted governmental intervention. While regulatory negotiation espouses these goals, the role of the state is very different; it is now only another "interested" party. Political legitimacy changes from the accountability and publicness of the process to participatory-based consensus. The agency withdraws from a more direct policing role. In Harrington's view, this is a return to the minimalist state and interest group theory of politics: "Regulatory negotiation is an example of how the law in deregulation politics reconstitutes state-market relations. Enthusiasm for the concept of alternatives is being transformed into an increasingly privatized version of the traditional administrative-regulatory process" (Harrington 1988:310). Harrington says that this is more than a return to interest group liberalism; rather, it is a philosophy of regulation of autonomous corporate bargaining (Harrington 1988).

Harrington's critique illustrates the project of Continental reflexive law—the withdrawal of the bureaucratic-legal regime from colonizing the economic subsystem. Law would function as "constitution" rather than "medium." It would set the *framework* for the more direct participation of the interested parties (including the state) rather than dictate the results. Law would allow for functional differentiation to enhance the integrity of the respective subsystems.

Summary

Certain themes stand out in this short review of major concepts of legal thought. The first theme clusters around the idea of the limits of rules in accomplishing the substantive goals of the modern social welfare state. This is not to argue that rules have no place, but that rules cannot do all of the work. There are large areas of human interaction, and especially citizen-state interaction, where legal formalism becomes dysfunctional; it fails to achieve the instrumental goals of the rules themselves, and, in the process, it often distorts or destroys other valuable relations.

The second theme clusters around the idea of creating the conditions in which people, including bureaucrats, can work things out according to relevant, contextualized values and interests. There are strong conceptual affinities between those who argue for more cooperative styles of regulation, those who argue for a cooperative style of bargaining and negotiation, the communitarian feminists, and the Continental theorists. Space must be created within which creative, flexible resolutions can be explored by the immediate parties. As we shall see in the discussion of critical philosophy, Habermas's ideal speech situation is a vision of unconstrained dialogue. The communitarian feminists envision a dialectic relation between the individual and others, a dynamic process which is both constitutive and transformative. Rather than resolving conflicts through abstract rules, structures must be designed to facilitate feminist discourse rooted in context. This again does not deny the normative values of the social welfare state. Rather, it says that those values cannot be applied abstractly and mechanically; they have to be applied, at the ground level, by the parties themselves in their own relevant context.

Chapter 5
Modern/Postmodern Communitarian Ethics

How are people to govern their actions? Max Weber saw the growth of formal rationalization; our activities were to be increasingly governed by rational bureaucratic rules. It was not a happy picture; we would be trapped in the "iron cage" of hierarchy and domination. We have seen that while bureaucracy has grown apace, it has hardly done so with Weberian efficiency. Bureaucracies are large and oppressive, regulation is often clumsy and inept. Citizens are subject to a bewildering variety of rules, often from competing jurisdictions. Discretion permeates most bureaucratic organizations; this is especially true of the bureaucracies that deal with complex regulatory tasks at the field level.

The authors that we have reviewed thus far have taken various approaches to the problem of citizen encounters with bureaucracy. The classic, liberal legal approach struggles to suppress bureaucratic discretion that is equated with arbitrary power and makes citizens subject to the tyranny and the whim of officials. Liberals seek to control, if not eliminate, discretion through the rule of law—the application of clear substantive rules or, failing that, strict due process procedures. As we have seen, this view has been sharply challenged. At the very least, as contemporary research in organizational sociology and implementation has shown, it is futile to think that discretion in most bureaucracies, especially at the field level, can be sharply reduced or even controlled successfully from the top. The rule of law, as the liberal legalists would have it, is simply not a viable option.

But the authors that we have discussed go further; rather than deplore the existence of discretion, they argue that it is wrong to *try* to govern human relationships through rules, that discretion is not only necessary, but *desirable*. The reflexive law theorists want regulatory law to pull back, to allow people to interact without the impediments of what is inevitably dysfunctional law. The communitarian feminists view the creation of space as essential for the caring, nurturing communication of femaleness. Those who argue for cooperative styles of regulation, alternative dispute resolution, and the problem-solving style of negotiation also view discretion affirmatively.

The liberal legalists worried about two problems—values and power. Values were to be discovered either through the utilitarian calculus or Kantian-based ontological rights. Whose values should prevail? Whether utilitarian or Kantian, the state would not choose. Rather, the task of the state would be to provide a neutral framework. Under utilitarianism, the ends, the good life, would be the sum of the preferences. The Kantians reject utilitarianism as a basis of moral law; its instrumentalism does not provide sufficient protection for freedom and rights and treats individuals as means to the happiness of others rather than as ends in themselves. The Kantians take rights much more seriously, but it is still fundamental to the preservation of these individually based rights that the state remain neutral; they cannot be overridden for the general welfare. As Michael Sandel puts it, the Kantian liberals draw a distinction between the "right" and the "good" (Sandel 1982). Neither utilitarians nor Kantians can agree either on what values are fundamental or on what frameworks are appropriate to enhance those values. Through the bargaining of pluralism, the political community would agree upon certain values, and these would be enacted into law (Sandel).

The other problem for liberals is the issue of power. Laws are not always clear, and people, including officials, cannot always be counted on to be law-abiding. How are the weak to protect themselves in the day-to-day dealings with officials? The liberal answer to this question is that the rule of law is the substantive restraint on all, citizens and officials alike; procedural due process is the mechanism by which the weak can protect themselves from the law-breaking powerful.

As we have seen, the legal aspect of the liberal legal program has been under serious attack as far back as legal realism; today, its ethical basis is also under attack. The liberal conception of the individual has been challenged on the ground that it does not give sufficient attention to the claims of citizenship and community. The rights-based ethic conceives of the individual as capable of standing back, assessing, and then choosing the good; the self is not defined by its goals and interests. The communitarians deny that people are so detached from goals and interests; rather, our roles are at least partly constitutive of ourselves. We are at least partly defined by our communities, their history, traditions, their goals and interests (Sandel). The communitarian feminists, we have seen, claim that personhood is constructed through social interaction (R. West).

But how, then, are decisions to be made? What are the ethical implications of abandoning the search for agreed-upon values, the utilitarian calculus, or fundamental rights? What does it mean to say that we are "partly" constituted by our social roles? All of the authors that we have reviewed who argue for governance through flexible, cooperative, communicative interaction emphasize the desirability, indeed the necessity, to take account of the other. But how are values decided in the community, and what about the issue of power?

Dialogism: The Communitarian Vision

In his book *Beyond Objectivism and Relativism: Science, Hermeneutics, and Praxis,* Richard Bernstein addresses the value question. What are the ethical implications of a modern/postmodern communitarian vision? Bernstein reviews and synthesizes what he believes to be a common vision among four contemporary influential philosophers—Hans-Georg Gadamer, Habermas, Richard Rorty, and Hannah Arendt. The common vision concerns the ethical considerations in the dialogical character of human existence. I will argue that these ethical considerations are the implicit foundation for several of the authors' positions that have been discussed in prior chapters. The call for cooperation in regulation, different styles of dispute resolution and bargaining, trust in human service organizations, and a communitarian feminist program are based in varying degrees on the ethical considerations of what Bernstein calls "dialogism." However, while Bernstein (and his four philosophers) think that there are strong ethical values in dialogism, they do not address in any systematic way the issue of power. The ethical considerations in dialogism are discussed in this chapter; the issues of structure and power are discussed in the next chapter in the context of four specific examples.

Bernstein's objective is to move beyond the objectivist/relativist debate, to ground human rationality in dialogism, with the idea that it is possible for people to reach agreement on values when there is extended, uncoerced, open conversation. Values, positions, agreements, and action can be reached without adopting either objectivism or radical skepticism. Objectivism is the belief that there is some permanent, ahistorical matrix or framework, some Archimedean point, which is the ultimate measure or test of rationality, knowledge, truth, goodness, and reality. The metaphysical or epistemological distinction between subject and object is the modern form of objectivism. "What is 'out there' (objective) is presumed to be independent of us (subjects); knowledge is achieved when a subject correctly mirrors or represents objective reality" (Bernstein 1985:8).

Relativists deny an overarching substantive framework or single metalanguage by which we can compare competing ethical values. Rather, concepts such as rationality, reality, the good, and so forth, can only be understood as relative to specific societies, cultures, or theoretical concepts. Every belief on any topic is as good as every other. This view has also been called "decisionism," which holds that moral propositions are founded only on individual choices and commitments. According to decisionism, there is a distinction between reason and choice; reason cannot help in the selection of specific values, it can only help to attain those values. Relativists, while denying the possibility of an ahistorical matrix, do allow for the possibility of shared moral standards which, at any particular historical moment, could have the appearance of being objective and universal; but the relativists would argue that such standards are in fact contextual and will change in the historical perspective (Cornell 1985).

The history of philosophy, according to Bernstein, has been fixated on the conflict between objectivism and relativism—called the Cartesian anxiety—that either there is some foundational, objective support for our being and knowledge, or there is only chaos. The paradigmatic example, of course, has been the physical sciences, where rationality has been defined in terms of rigorous empiricism and deductive reasoning. Postempirical philosophy of science has challenged that view. Focusing on the work of Thomas Kuhn, philosophers of science argue that the conventional epistemological model of how, in fact, science proceeds is false. "Normal" science may proceed pursuant to the strict canons of positivism, but when rival paradigms develop, there are, in fact, no fixed, ahistorical methods of selection; rather, different forms of rationality are employed. Communities of scientists reflect and eventually reach a consensus on which paradigm is supported by the best evidence. This is a form of rationality, but it is a form that is analogous to *phronesis:*

It is a type of reasoning in which there is a mediation between general principles and a concrete particular situation that requires choice and decision. In forming such a judgment there are no determinate technical rules by which a particular can simply be subsumed under that which is general or universal. What is required is an interpretation and specification of universals that are appropriate to this particular situation. (Bernstein 1985:54)

Phronesis, or practical knowledge, as developed by Aristotle referred to the discussions and deliberations that took place in the Greek cities, the *polis*. So too, argues Kuhn, the judgment and rational deliberations over rival paradigms take place and are "shaped by the social practices of the relevant scientific community" (Bernstein 1985:54). Choice is a judgmental activity. While such judgments are supported by reasons, they also require imagination, interpretation, and the weighing of alternatives. Supporting reasons themselves are not immutable; they vary over time and over the course of scientific development (Bernstein 1985: 54). Scientific theories are often based on multiple strands of evidence, hunches, and arguments, no one of which would be sufficient in itself to establish the hypothesis, but taken together they provide the basis for a rational belief in one particular choice. It is only in a "community of inquirers," a "critical community," that the strength of such multiple arguments can be tested (Bernstein 1985:69).

Bernstein makes two points from this example. Kuhn is describing what, in fact, is the scientific practice when scientists are confronted by "extraordinary science." The second point, which is the important one for our purposes, is the nature of the process. A consensus emerges from the relevant scientific community; there is discussion, there is dialogue. But, the methodology is *rational* in the sense that evidence is carefully examined and weighed; it is not rigorously empirical, the kind of methodology that one associates with experimentation and the deductive reasoning in "normal" science. Rather, rationality is essentially dialogic and intersubjective. Because rigorous, empiricist, normal science cannot give the answer, what is called for is *judgment*. This is not "objectivist" in the sense that the subject is separated from the object: there is an indissoluble link between the thinking subject (the scientists) and nature. On the other hand, scientific practice is also not relativist, argues Bernstein. It is a fallacy to think that because there are no determinate rules for distinguishing between interpretations, that there is no rational way to make comparative practical judgments (Bernstein 1985:91).

What is the process, then, by which people interpret nature and make judgments? Hermeneutics, the philosophy of interpretation, offers an explanation of how we arrive at knowledge and truth. While its most important contemporary explication, *Truth and Method*, by Hans-Georg Gadamer (in Bernstein, ed., 1985), deals almost exclusively with art and literature, hermeneutics has become extremely influential in the contemporary philosophy of ethics and social science.

Gadamer seeks to connect hermeneutics with the tradition of practical philosophy. He argues that understanding, interpretation, and application are all internally related; each act of one necessarily involves the others, and it is application that provides the link between hermeneutics and the tradition of practical philosophy. There is a dynamic interaction between the work of art and the spectator. A work of art needs an interpreter, someone to share it, "someone upon whom the work of art makes a claim" (Bernstein 1985:122). In doing this, in participating in the work of art, we carry with us our "prejudices." By this, Gadamer means that our reason and understanding cannot be free from our historical, contextual beings. Our prejudices (Bernstein prefers the less pejorative "prejudgments") are constitutive. By opening ourselves up to the work of art, by entering into a dialogue with that which is alien to us, which makes a claim upon us, we can discover which of our prejudices are blinding and which are enabling. It is the interaction between our historically situated enabling prejudices and the "thing" which enables us to understand the "thing" (Bernstein 1985:137). "Hermeneutics sees history as a living dialogue between past, present, and future, and seeks patiently to remove obstacles to this endless mutual communication" (Eagleton 1983:73). Because prejudices are constitutive, the project will never be complete, we will never be able to attain full and complete knowledge. "We are always understanding and interpreting in light of our anticipatory prejudgments and prejudices which are themselves changing in the course of history. To understand is always to understand *differently*" (emphasis original, Bernstein 1985:139).

The relation between hermeneutics and practical philosophy or *praxis* arises out of the inextricable connection between the theoretical and the practical in all understanding, interpretation, and application. The dialogue between our constitutive prejudgments and the "things themselves," the simultaneous blending of understanding, interpretation, and application into understanding, is, according to Gadamer, both ontological and universal; it underlies all human activity. Because language is the medium of all understanding and tradition, there is no "objective knowledge" that is detached from one's self. This model of understanding is dialogical, practical, and communal. There is choice, deliberation, interpretation, and the weighing of universal criteria. The dialogue is central to Gadamer's hermeneutics. The dialogue is the process of two people coming to understand each other. A dialogue entails a common bond, mutual respect, a genuine listening, an openness to testing our own opinions. It is in the dialogical community that *phronesis* can be practiced (Bernstein 1985:174).

Gadamer thinks that the greatest danger to hermeneutical understanding arises from our abdication to experts, the purveyors of technical knowledge, to whom citizens have forfeited their "noblest task"—"decision-making according to one's own responsibility"

(Bernstein 1985:159). When citizens reclaim that noble task, they will have achieved freedom; freedom is realized only when there is authentic mutual recognition among individuals. But there will also be community. People who understand "cannot stand apart." There will be friendship and solidarity.

Habermas's project is to elaborate a comprehensive, empirical, scientific theory of rationality based on communicative action. He seeks to define the universal conditions required for human communication, a "universal pragmatics" (Bernstein, ed., 1985:16). Universal conditions are necessary, he believes, if we are to rationally ground a critical theory of society; otherwise, criticism would only become ad hoc, and would, in fact, be neoconservative.

Communicative action is action that is oriented to mutual understanding. This is to be distinguished from instrumental or social strategic action, which is oriented toward success. The goal of communicative action is an agreement based on intersubjective, mutual, reciprocal understanding, shared knowledge, and mutual trust with one another (Bernstein, ed., 1985).

There are two major ideas in Habermas's theory of communication and language. First, Habermas argues that all speech acts contain four implicit validity claims: (1) comprehensibility—that what is said is intelligible; (2) that the proposition or the factual assertions are true; (3) that the speaker is truthful in the sense that she is justified in making the statements; and (4) that the speaker is sincere. Communicative rationality signifies a mode of raising and accepting the validity claims. It is a reflexive conception of human communication in that the validity claims can *only* emerge and be redeemed within human discourse (Giddens 1985; Wellmer 1985). Habermas's second idea is that the use of language presumes an "ideal speech situation": "that form of discourse in which there is no other compulsion but the compulsion of argumentation itself; where there is genuine symmetry among the participants involved, allowing a universal interchangeability of dialogue roles; where no form of domination exists" (Bernstein 1976:212). It is in such "undistorted communication" that the speaker can defend all four validity claims (Giddens:128–129). Discourse suspends judgment on whether the validity claims are to be redeemed. There are structural barriers in society that systematically distort dialogue and communication; the task is to remove such blocking and distorting barriers.

Habermas believes that norms can only be validated by participants in practical discourse. The process is essentially Socratic but the validity of norms is rationally based. "In these validity claims, communication theory can locate a gentle but obstinate, a never silent although seldom redeemed claim to reason, a claim that must be recognized de facto whenever and wherever there is to be consensual action" (Bernstein 1985:191).

Bernstein reminds us that it is important to recognize Habermas's theory of communicative action contemplates *procedural rationality* rather than *substantive rationality*. Habermas is talking about general structures of communication; he does not specify an ideal society or the contents of the good life. The redemption of validity claims through dialogue contemplates the importance of plurality (Bernstein 1985:192).

While other proponents of dialogism make a similar point, it should be noted that the virtues of dialogism are considered to be constituent aspects of the good life. Cornell, for example, argues that while dialogism (as well as liberalism) cannot give us a "full vision" of the good, the civic virtues that are necessary for dialogism are "at least a component part of an adequate vision of the good" (Cornell 1985:376). Bernstein says that it is only through dialogue that one achieves self-reflection that is emancipatory (Bernstein 1985).

Although Habermas argues for the rationality potential of communicative action, he does not think that it can carry the whole load of integration in post-traditional societies. Additional forms of systemic integration (economic and bureaucratic rationalization) must be complementary. The life-worlds of communicative action and social systems presuppose each other. They are integrated by different forms of rationality. The rationality of systems is purposive; the rationality of the life-world is communicative. As discussed in Chapter 4, Habermas thinks that we are threatened today by processes of system rationality (the colonization of the life-world; Bernstein 1985). In an emancipated society, the life-world would no longer be subjected to the imperatives of system maintenance; rather, the life-world would subject the systemic mechanisms to the needs of people coordinated through communicative action. In Habermas's idealized life-world, there is free agreement. Coordination through such agreements is his all-pervasive principle. It is the normative core of democratic consensus (Wellmer).

Habermas does not believe that there is any underlying historical necessity for the systematic destruction of the life-world. Rather, what is happening in modern society is the selective process of encroachment by purposive rationality, which destroys and deforms the life-world. What is called for is the achievement of a proper balance between the legitimate demands of systemic rationalization and communicative rationalization (Bernstein 1985).

Habermas has been criticized for his claim that his theory of communicative action is scientifically based. Some argue that this is yet another futile attempt to ground rationality transcendentally. Bernstein argues for another reading of Habermas—as pragmatic, interpretative dialectics. There is a moral-political intention in Habermas's work; he would have us overcome the systematic distortions to communication, to approach the ideal speech situation in which there is reciprocal dialogue, and in which there would be autonomy and respect and solidarity. Redeeming the universal, normative validity claims ought to be the goal of our everyday practices and institutions (Bernstein 1985).

Richard Rorty is one of Habermas's critics. But in many important respects, Rorty and Habermas are in agreement, especially on the value of democratic institutions, how these institutions ought to be improved, and on what constitutes oppression. Rorty's definition of a liberal society is similar to Habermas's: "A liberal society is one which is content to call 'true' (or 'right' or 'just') whatever the outcome of undistorted communication happens to be, whatever view wins in a free and open encounter" (Rorty 1989:67). He objects to Habermas's conviction that a democratic society must embody the universalism of the Enlightenment; he says that Habermas's theory of communicative reason is only an updating of rationalism. While Rorty is sympathetic to the idea or the goal of undistorted communication, he is suspicious of any kind of universal *theory* of communication. He thinks that even appeals to something like a rational consensus can be regressive and stifling, and contests the view that a transcendental or universalistic standpoint is necessary for liberal social criticism. Instead of trying to ground a universal theory, Rorty says attention should focus on the structures that are currently distorting our communication (Rorty 1985). According to Rorty, the Socratic virtues are moral virtues only. While Gadamer and Habermas believe that philosophical hermeneutics or universal pragmatics can still provide some kind of support for a metaphysical or epistemological grounding, Rorty is "postmodern" in the sense that he wants to root out the last vestiges of metaphysics (Bernstein 1985).

Nevertheless, as Bernstein argues, Rorty's "subtext," his defense of pragmatism, is the defense of the Socratic virtues—the willingness to take conversation seriously. His utopia is the liberal society—"one whose ideals can be fulfilled by persuasion rather than force, by reform rather than revolution, by the free and open encounters of present linguistic and other practices with suggestions for new practices. But this is to say that an ideal liberal society is one which has no purpose except freedom, no goal except a willingness to see how such encounters go and to abide by the outcome" (Rorty 1989:60). In this important pragmatic sense, his idea is quite similar to Gadamer and Habermas (Bernstein 1985). Although Bernstein is careful to note that there are important differences between Gadamer, Habermas, and Rorty, "all three are concerned to show us what is vital to the human project and to give a sense of what dialogue, conversation, questioning, solidarity, and community mean. All three stress the multiple ways in which these are threatened in the contemporary world" (Bernstein 1985:206).

The fourth modern philosopher that Bernstein discusses is Hannah Arendt. Her connection with the others lies in her discussion of the type of public space that is created when two people act together. Debate, according to Arendt, is a form of action, and for her, it "'constitutes the very essence of political life,' it is the highest form of the *vita activa*" (Bernstein 1985:207). Action and speech are intrinsically political activities requiring the existence of public space, for that is where individuals encounter each other and reveal who they are. Persuasion only comes about as the result of free and open debate among equals. Freedom consists of two individuals debating, in public spaces, and participating in the determination of civic life. Power is created through participation. Power, freedom, equality, speech, and action are, thus, "essentially intersubjective and communicative; [they come] into existence only in the mutual creation of a public space in between individuals" (Bernstein 1985:210).

The common threads in all of the works of these writers, says Bernstein, are "the central themes of dialogue, conversation, undistorted communication, communal judgment, and the type of rational wooing that can take place when individuals confront each other as equals and participants" (Bernstein 1985:223). This commonality holds the possibility that generalized interests will emerge in the course of conversation (Cornell 1987a).

Some Preliminary Questions

The dialogism project is founded on community, but what kind of community? What concept is there of the community and the individual? In classic liberalism, people, of course, interact, often in close connection for long periods of time. How does the concept of the community among the dialogians differ from liberal interaction?

Michael Sandel, in *Liberalism and the Limits of Justice,* distinguishes between three conceptions of community. Two are discussed by Rawls. One is an *instrumental* community, in which individuals cooperate only to achieve their own private ends; cooperation is a necessary burden. Rawls's view of community is one in which cooperation can be a good in itself; there are shared common ends. This is the *sentimental* community. The sense of community is *partly* internal—partly, says Sandel, because of Rawls's concept of the antecedent individual, the subject of cooperation. Rawls is a Kantian liberal, and Kantian liberals draw a distinction between the right and the good. Thus, Rawls's sentimental community, while it encompasses shared ends, cannot be *constitutive* because it would span the boundary between the antecedent liberal self and the good (Sandel:149).

The third conception of community, the strong sense of community, is what Sandel calls a *constitutive conception*. He defines it as follows:

A theory of community whose province extended to the subject as well as the object of motivation would be individualistic in neither the conventional sense nor in Rawls'. It would resemble Rawls' conception in that the sense of community would be manifest in the aims and values of the participants—as fraternal sentiments and fellow-feeling, for example—but would differ from Rawls' conception in that community would describe not just a *feeling* but a mode of self-understanding partly constitutive of the agent's identity. On this strong view... members of a society... conceive their identity—the subject and not just the object of their feelings and aspirations—as defined to some extent by the community of which they are a part. For them, community describes not just what they *have* as fellow citizens but also what they *are*, not a relationship they choose (as in a voluntary association) but an attachment they discover, not merely an attribute but a constituent of their identity. (Sandel:150, 173; emphasis original)

The proponents of the constitutive community question the modern liberal conception of the "freely choosing individual." Like the communitarian feminists, they believe that personhood cannot be conceived apart from social relationships. Communitarians deny that the self can be wholly detached from its aims and attachments. We are partly constituted, according to Sandel, by the communities in which we live (Sandel).

Sandel argues that these very different conceptions of the individual—"unencumbered selves and situated" selves—lead to very different politics. The Kantians, the party of rights, divide along egalitarian and libertarian lines, but worry about the "politics of the common good" (Baker 1985). The modern state is not the Greek *polis*, and "any attempt to govern by a vision of the good is likely to lead to a slippery slope of totalitarian temptations" (Young). According to Marilyn Friedman "[C]ommunitarian philosophy as a whole is a perilous ally for feminist theory. Communitarians invoke a model of community which is focused particularly on families, neighborhoods, and nations. These sorts of communities have harbored social roles and structures which have been highly oppressive for women" (Friedman:277). She favors friendships and "urban relationships." The communitarians, on the other hand, believe that because of the dislocations and confusions of the atomized, anomic self and because common involvement has withered, we are vulnerable to mass politics and totalitarianism.

The dialogists and the constitutive communitarians decry individualism as conceived by classic liberalism. At the same time, they draw back from the full implications of community. They, too, want to preserve some measure of autonomy. Their concept is *partial;* they speak in qualifications—their favorite adverb is "partly." In Sandel's definition of communitarians, he twice uses "partly"—our roles are only "partly" constitutive; we are only "partly" defined by our communities. Alasdair MacIntyre has a similar qualification. He argues that although we are embedded in our communities, from which we derive our identities, and even though "the self has to find its moral identity in and through its membership in communities such as those of the family, the neighborhood, the city and the tribe," it does not follow "that the self has to accept the moral *limitations* of the particularity of those forms of community." Rather, "it is in moving forward from such particularity that the search for the good, for the universal, consists" (MacIntyre 1984:143; emphasis original).

Drucilla Cornell, following the analysis of Bernstein, Gadamer, and Habermas (and the communitarian feminists), argues that the core of dialogism transcends the dichotomy between sameness and difference: "symmetric reciprocity between participants" entails "mutually dependent moments in a conversational relationship." But while "we are left with a decentered subject, relational at its core, this... however, does not dissolve the self totally in an all-encompassing community" (Cornell 1985:298). Seeking to preserve the values of autonomy and equality in dialogism, Cornell states: "[A] sphere of rights would still have a place, but it would no longer serve primarily to maintain a radical separation between the individual and the community. The very idea of right would be redefined to emphasize what I would call participatory rights" (Cornell 1985:374).

Habermas is deeply suspicious of what he calls romantic or neo-romantic tendencies that imagine a "new" organic wholeness where differences are overcome (see Young). He opposes the bias that humans must not only be reconciled with each other but also with nature, or that cultural differentiation must inevitably result in alienation and reification, and says that we can accept differentiation and still seek ways to integrate and harmonize our everyday lives. As previously stated, Habermas believes that a proper balance can be struck between the legitimate demands of social systems and the life-world (Bernstein 1985).

But what does "partly constitutive" mean? How is this different from Rawls's shared ends, or from feelings (Baker)? How does MacIntyre's situated self separate itself to observe, decide, and move forward from the moral limitations of its community? The communitarians want to preserve some freedom of choice, but what defines the difference? We will return to these questions shortly.

Bernstein notes that with the communitarians, there is an incipient prior sense of community. This tends to assume the *ability* of people to participate, a point that draws sharp criticism from Terry Eagleton:

Hermeneutics sees history as a living dialogue between past, present and future, and seeks patiently to remove obstacles to this endless mutual communication. [But it fails to] come to terms with the problem of ideology—with the fact that the unending "dialogue" of human history is as often as not a monologue by the powerful to the powerless, or that if it is indeed a "dialogue" then the partners—men and women, for example—hardly occupy equal positions. It refuses to recognize that discourse is always caught up with a power which may be by no means benign. (Eagleton:73)

Bernstein constructs a similar criticism of Gadamer. While Gadamer stresses the contemporary threat of expertise (*technē*) to dialogism, Bernstein thinks that the more important danger arises out of domination and power.

To insist that there are real possibilities in any society [to exemplify the virtues of Socrates, Plato, and Aristotle] no matter how just or unjust the society may be, is not yet to confront a crucial question—the question of what material, social, and political conditions need to be concretely realized in order to encourage the flourishing of *phronesis* in all citizens. (Bernstein 1985:157)

Bernstein recognizes the practical difficulties of trying to realize dialogism in present society, "considering the fragile conditions that are required for genuine dialogue and conversation." Nevertheless, he argues that dialogism can help us define our practical, political task. The willingness to listen can become a "powerful regulative ideal that can orient our practical and political lives.... [It] can and should give practical orientation to our lives" (Bernstein 1985: 162–163). We should not despair. "What we desperately need today is to learn to think and act more like the fox than the hedgehog—

to seize upon those experiences and struggles in which there are still the glimmerings of solidarity and the promise of dialogical communities in which there can be genuine mutual participation and where reciprocal wooing and persuasion can prevail" (Bernstein 1985:227–228).

But we are still left uncertain as to how to find, construct, nurture, and preserve dialogical communities in the modern state. Dialogism may be a "powerful regulative ideal that can orient our practical and political lives," but what is it, and what are the conditions for its existence?

What Kind of Community?

It is now time to address the two issues that have been left hanging—power and the quality of participation. On the issue of power, liberals assume a presocial, autonomous person. Dialogue necessarily entails two autonomous participants, individuals capable of talking and listening, and of self-determination. Therefore, in order for there to be a dialogue, unequal participants must be empowered. As Rawls points out, the *quality* of participation can be purely *instrumental*, where cooperation is a necessity, or *sentimental*, where the affective aspects of cooperation are goods in themselves.

Communitarians conflate the issues of power and the quality of participation by arguing that since the self is defined by the social context, the process of dialogue itself is empowering; as the barriers to communication are removed, there is, by definition, a move toward equality because the participants become equal moral agents.

The dialogue, it will be recalled, is much more than an instrumental conversation. It is extended, uncoerced, and open; it entails a common bond, mutual respect, and genuine listening. This kind of interaction is both transformative and constitutive: transformative, in that there is empowerment—a previously powerless person is now an equal moral agent; constitutive, in that ideology is not separate from action, but is integral to social practices. Ideology defines experiences and social relationships. It constructs reality. "There is no social world except as it is lived and experienced, and events become socially meaningful only when they are interpreted." Thus, "ideology is constitutive, in that ideas about an event or relationship define that activity, much as the rules about a game define a mover or a victory in that game" (Merry 1986:254). Through the process of dialogue, the previously powerless person now has a different self-concept, and a different concept of others and the relationship. In this sense, the communitarian dialogue is constitutive of the participants.

The nature of the dialogical community can be clarified by analyzing the concept of trust. The idea of trust runs throughout this entire argument. Hawkins's water pollution control inspectors and manufacturers develop a certain amount of trust. Hasenfeld argues that the caseworker-client interaction cannot be successful unless there is a certain amount of mutual trust. The communitarian feminists, the dialogians, and those who see deeper connections with alternative dispute resolution include trust as one of the important humanistic values. Habermas's validity claims are based, in part, on trust. What do we mean by trust?

In the philosophical literature, the most systematic treatment of trust that I am aware of is Annette Baier's article "Trust and Antitrust" (1986). She begins by noting that many forms of cooperative behavior involve trust. We trust not only intimates, but also strangers. We trust strangers to leave us alone, to respect our autonomy. Trust, according to Niklas Luhmann, is necessary to reduce the complexities of life (Luhmann 1980:4).

Baier draws a distinction between merely relying on the dependable habits of others and trusting; the latter relies on *goodwill*. But this means that when one relies on another's goodwill, one becomes vulnerable to the limits of that goodwill. But while there is the opportunity to harm the trusting person, there is also the confidence that this will not happen. But if trust involves vulnerability, why, asks Baier, do we place ourselves in such positions? We leave things that we value under the control of others because we need their help in creating or sustaining those things that we value—for example, our lives, health, reputation, children, as well as intrinsically shared goods such as conversation, entertainment, work, and social and political life.

Trust involves discretion. Normal people, says Baier, generally know the limits of their trust. When we confide our troubles to a friend, the friend will usually know how to take care of that confidence; she also will know that taking active steps to alleviate the trouble may be over the limits.

Discretion increases vulnerability; it allows for both abuse and concealment. Concealment is present in many forms of trust. We trust our surgeon and plumber to use their discretion competently and with our best interests at heart; yet, they have the ability to conceal their mistakes or ill will behind the pretense of an honest exercise in judgment, thereby maintaining our trust and increasing our vulnerability. Trust can be explicit, but often it is not. Rather, it often "grows up slowly and imperceptibly. . . . Trust can come with no beginnings, with gradual as well as sudden beginnings, and with various degrees of self-consciousness, voluntariness, and expressiveness" (Baier:240). Trust can be unconscious or conscious and cultivated. But Baier doubts that we can trust at will; we usually already trust someone, and efforts to enhance trust are usually designed to prevent distrust.

Trust also involves power; more specifically, it alters power relationships. Baier strongly emphasizes the importance of understanding trust in *unequal* relationships. The infant-parent trust relationship is both innate and fragile in that it does not need to be won, but it can be destroyed. Though this is an example of extreme dependency and unequal vulnerability, trust is to some extent mutual; the parent also is "vulnerable to the child's at first insignificant but ever-increasing power, including power as one trusted by the parent" (Baier:242).

The parent supplies the child with nutrition, shelter, health, clothing, love. As the child becomes more self-conscious, she can expect the parent to keep supplying those goods because of the concept of *common goods:* the goods that the parents supply to the child are presumably also goods to the parents. Harm to these goods would be self-harm. "The best reason for confidence in another's good care of what one cares about is that it is a common good" (Baier:243). There may not be agreement on how best to take care of that common good, but the fact that it is common decreases the likelihood of ill will.

Baier distinguishes trust from contract, a distinction that illuminates the difference between instrumental cooperation and dialogism. Trust in the parent-child relationship is not contractual. Trust and vulnerabilities become increasingly mutual with the passage of time, and adult children may become responsible for their parents. But this later relationship, however contractual it may be, does not transform the *initial* trust and trustworthiness into a contractual exchange. The childhood relation may be a moral reason, says Baier, for taking care of one's parents; but it is not consideration (Held).

Nevertheless, making contracts or promises implicitly includes an invitation to trust; this is real, voluntary trusting. However, while contracts and promises create trust, Baier points out that they do not capture the full variety and moral dimensions of trust. Contracts are mainly used by adults who are not intimate with each other, who see one another as more or less equal in power. It is "all along an elite right, possessed only by those with a certain social status.... Contract is a device for traders, entrepreneurs, and capitalists, not for children, servants, indentured wives, and slaves" (Baier:247). When the have-nots, dependent people, "are taken seriously as moral subjects and agents," contracts constituting voluntary agreements and trust in others to keep their agreements "must be moved from the center to the moral periphery" (Baier:247). A moral code that presupposes equality when the participants are, in fact, unequal is at best nonfunctional and, more likely, "an offensive pretense of equality as a substitute for its actuality" (Baier:249).

Moreover, equality is not a goal in all relationships; we need a morality to guide us in dealings with those who are dependent or who have intimate relationships. Virginia Held, arguing a feminist alternative to contractual equality, makes this point in discussing the idea of equality between mother and child: "Parents and children should not have equal rights in the sense that what they are entitled to decide or to do or to have should be the same.... But every member of a family is worthy of equal respect and consideration. Each person in a family is as important as a person as every other" (Held 1987:128).

When is a given form of trust morally decent? Baier proposes a moral test in terms of *expressibility*—can the trust relationship survive the knowledge of what the parties are relying on to continue the relationship? Baier uses the example of the trust that an old-fashioned husband has in his wife for the care of their child. The basis for trust is that the parents care about the "same good"—the child's happiness. As long as there are not radical disagreements as to how to care for the child, the husband can trust the discretion of the wife to make the day-to-day decisions. On the other hand, the knowledge that the wife's values seriously conflict with those of the husband, and that the wife is willing to sacrifice the husband's concerns for her concerns and those of the child, would undermine the trust.

Trusting is rational; it depends on an assessment of the other's *goodwill*. If the husband believes that the wife is only conforming to his wishes to avoid sanctions, then he will have to rely on threats rather than trust. The wife also makes a rational calculation; she will keep the trust as long as she thinks that the goods preserved by the trust are more important than those she would have by breaking or abusing the trust. The goods, of course, can include a lot more than the child's goods—love, mutual trust for its own sake, support, security, or the avoidance of sanctions.

Rational, or sensible trust, then, can exist in a variety of situations where the participants are, in fact, suspicious of each other. Threats and concealment can keep the relationship going. This kind of trust, says Baier, is "morally rotten." Baier applies the expressibility test to determine the moral basis of trust. If the husband learns that the wife relies on his blindness or gullibility, that knowledge helps change the husband's sight. If the wife learns that the husband relies on her fear of sanctions or her ignorance to keep her trustworthy, she, too, will begin to change and become more untrustworthy. Thus,

[a] trust relationship is morally bad to the extent that either party relies on qualities in the other which would be weakened by the knowledge that the other relies on them. Where each relies on the other's love, or concern for some *common good or professional pride in competent discharge of responsibility,* knowledge of what the other is relying on in one need not undermine but will more likely strengthen those relied-on features. (Baier:256; emphasis added)

The moral test requires that the relationship survive when the psychological states relevant to continuing the relations, such as "love, fear, ignorance, sense of powerlessness, good nature, inattention," are made explicit. Summing up, Baier's definition is as follows:

trust is morally decent only if, in addition to whatever else is entrusted, knowledge of each party's reasons for confident reliance on the other to continue the relationship could in principle also be entrusted—since mutual knowledge would be itself a good, not a threat to the other goods. To the extent that mutual reliance can be accompanied by mutual knowledge of the conditions for that reliance, trust is above suspicion, and trustworthiness a nonsuspect virtue. (Baier:259–260)

Baier's morally decent trust fits the ethical prescriptions of dialogism—there are mutual respect, common bonds, genuine listening, and openness. There is equal moral agency between unequal participants—children, servants, "indentured" wives, and slaves. Is this, then, a community in the strong sense? Are these communities different from John Rawls's instrumental or sentimental communities?

In a section of *A Theory of Justice* titled "The Morality of Association," Rawls talks about the moral standards that are appropriate to the individual's role in various associations—for example, family, school, neighborhood, and various adult statuses. The ideals are contextual: while each person relates differently to the association, each member gradually learns the point of view of others, to see things from their perspective, a necessary event if we are to understand and assess the actions and intentions of others. The ability to perceive the other person, however, is not sufficient; after all, manipulative and exploitive people also do this. Rather, one has to develop "friendly feelings towards one's associates, together with feelings of trust and confidence. . . . Thus, if those engaged in a system of social cooperation regularly act with evident intention to uphold its just (or fair) rules, bonds of friendship and mutual trust tend to develop among them, thereby holding them ever more securely to the scheme" (Rawls:470). When the arrangements of an association are recognized to be just, all of the members benefit from its activities, and the conduct of each member is to the advantage of all.

There is much in Rawls's conception that would be compatible with Baier's moral trust. Rawls distinguishes between the manipulator and exploiter. His cooperative virtues—justice, fairness, fidelity, integrity, impartiality—are certainly moral virtues. His morality of association, in which we strive to put ourselves in the place of others, could be construed as altering power relations. Changing practices and ideologies could be constitutive and transformative. Baker, for example, thinks that the positions of Rawls and Habermas are parallel in their efforts "to find conditions of interaction in which attempts to reach agreement through uncoerced communicative action can succeed" (Baker:901).

Sandel, on the other hand, thinks that there are real differences between Rawls's community and community in the strong sense. Even though cooperative behavior is a shared end (a common good), it is still individualistic. Rawls does say, "But finally, having understood another's situation, it still remains for us to regulate our own conduct in the appropriate way by reference to it" (Rawls:468). The dialogians, the communitarian feminists, and strong communitarians favor some measure of autonomy; relations remain reflexive, at least to some degree. Sandel, however, thinks that there are important differences between associations based on Kantian principles and community in the strong sense. A strong community, argues Sandel, is defined by more than common sentiments and aims; rather, it is how the subjects conceive of their identity:

the subject and not just the object of their feelings and aspirations—as defined to some extent by the community of which they are a part. For them, community describes not just what they *have* as fellow citizens but also what they *are*, not a relationship they choose (as in a voluntary association) but an attachment they discover, not merely an attribute but a constituent of their identity. (Sandel:150; emphasis original)

Sandel further states that

the moral vocabulary of community in the strong sense cannot in all cases be captured by a conception that "in its theoretical basis is individualistic." Thus a "community" cannot always be translated without loss to an "association," nor an "attachment" to a "relationship," nor "sharing" to "reciprocating," nor "participation" to "co-operation," nor what is "common" to what is "collective." ... [W]hile "reciprocity" implies a principle of exchange and hence a plurality of agents, the notion of "sharing" may suggest a solidarity such that no exchange need be involved, as in sharing a joke, or an aspiration, or an understanding. And while "association" and "cooperation" typically presuppose the antecedent plurality of those who join together to associate or co-operate, "community" and "participation" may describe a form of life in which the members find themselves commonly situated "to begin with," their commonality consisting less in the relationship they have entered than in attachments they have found. (Sandel:151–152)

The differences between Rawls and Sandel lie in their fundamentally different conceptions of the self—between the self of deontological liberalism that chooses its ends and the communitarian self that discovers its ends through self-reflection (Baker; Cornell 1987b). The liberal self is prior to and detached from those constituent attachments that would provide the basis for choice. Sandel's self is situated "to begin with" in attachments that are already found; comprehension comes "through self-reflection and dialogue with fellow friends, who, because they understand the nature of their self-defining membership in a joint community, can know each other and help each other come to understand their common path to a fuller self-realization" (Goldstein:117).

Sandel's conception of the self follows a long line of rejection of Kantian liberalism. Bernstein and Rorty, for example, urge a renewed attention to the pragmatism of Dewey, who thought that it makes no sense to speak of individuals apart from or independent of their social context (Bernstein:1985).

The root differences between Rawls and Sandel are beyond the concerns of this book. What we are trying to explore is the possibilities of dialogism in the modern social welfare state; whether in certain situations people in significantly unequal situations can relate to each other as equal moral agents; whether clients and workers can be open, can listen to each other, and have mutual respect; whether there can be morally decent trust between dependent clients and social welfare bureaucracies. Such relationships would be both constitutive and transformative in that they would equalize power and change both ideology and practice. The moral values of the dialogians and the communitarian feminists become additional common goods—respect, honesty, autonomy, cooperation. Empowerment, based on trust, necessarily involves significant changes in beliefs about oneself and others.

The next chapter presents specific empirical examples drawn from informed consent in medicine, special education, community-based care for the frail, elderly poor, and water pollution control regulation. The ideas of the previous two chapters—cooperative-style regulation, alternative dispute resolution, reflexive law, communitarian feminists, and dialogical ethics—will be examined to see whether it is possible to establish a dialogical community in bureaucratic relationships.

Chapter 6
Four Examples in the Modern State

I will now examine the theories of cooperation, dialogism, and community in the context of four specific examples—informed consent in medicine, the education of handicapped children, long-term care for the frail, elderly poor, and the water pollution control regulation discussed in Chapter 2. Each example shows two different kinds of relationships between the citizen and the state. The dominant regime, which I call *legal-bureaucratic,* is characterized by formalism, hierarchy, and domination. Most citizen-state relations are regulated by the dominant regime. The exception in each example is characterized by equality and shared decision-making; I call this *participatory*. The theoretical literature will be used to help answer the following questions: Why have the regulatory fields developed along legal-bureaucratic lines? Why have the participatory exceptions developed? What are the constituent elements of participation? What does the theory tell us about the issues of *power* and the *quality of participation?* To what extent do the participatory exceptions illustrate dialogism? Is there autonomy and participation, or is there autonomy, participation, *and* community?

In the participatory exceptions, I will argue that there are the possibilities of a coherent theory of dialogism in the relationship between dependent people and the state. In the water pollution control example, there is cooperation but not dialogism. The concluding chapter will discuss the material and social conditions of dialogism in these relationships.

Informed Consent in Medical Ethics

As discussed in Chapter 2, the President's Commission for the Study of Ethical Problems in Medicine and Biomedical and Behavioral Research defines informed consent as a process of shared decision-making based upon mutual respect. Informed consent is based on the ethical values of personal well-being and self-determination; it is a mutual relationship. Patient choice, while fundamental, is not absolute; the patient is not entitled to insist on care that violates the deeply held values of the physician. Physicians are also autonomous and entitled to respect (President's Commission).

There are difficult issues that arise in the concept of informed consent. How much information should be disclosed? How much information would a reasonable person, or this particular person, want to know? Jay Katz argues that the process of mutual conversation must be built up patiently, gradually, and with great skill in order for both the physician and the patient to know what and why they are deciding. Informed consent raises the issues of competency, rationality, and voluntariness (Katz 1984).

As an abstract ideal, informed consent is a basic, agreed-upon value; it reflects our fundamental conceptions of human dignity. Why, then, is informed consent in medicine such a difficult and troublesome problem? Ever since its recorded history, the medical profession had been unalterably opposed to the idea of informed consent. While there are, no doubt, many mundane if not immoral reasons for this opposition, the principal reason is that a great many doctors do not believe that informed consent is therapeutically beneficial. The task of the physician is to provide the best, the most humane, care for the patient. Physicians believe that this task will be compromised if there is shared decision-making. Medicine is uncertain, even in the most routine procedures. Knowledge is esoteric. The condition of the patient is never static; as it evolves, different considerations become relevant. Physicians themselves often have a great deal of difficulty in sorting out the relevant information. How, then, can they convey this uncertainty to patients in a sensible manner?

Many physicians also feel that most patients lack the capacity to comprehend the information. They view patients as childlike, and, because of the anxiety, helplessness, and dependency that illness engenders, many patients do appear this way. Many patients want to believe in their doctors; they want reassurance, not conversations about uncertainties. Physicians believe that trust is necessary to the therapeutic relationship. To raise uncertainties with patients would cause unnecessary anxiety and lack of confidence; and, in the end, the patients simply would insist that the doctors do what they think "best." Physicians justify this acknowledged paternalism by citing traditional professional ethics—their devotion to service and to act in the patients' best interests. In sum, the doctor-patient relationship consists of a doctor who decides and presents a recommendation which the patient then accepts (Katz; President's Commission).

Other than the application of the law of battery, which was quite narrow, the law did not intervene until the mid-1950s when the term "informed consent" first appeared in an appellate decision. At issue was a new and risky procedure, and the American College of Surgeons, in an amicus brief, thought that patients should be made aware. Thereafter, in a series of cases, courts attempted to define more precisely the duties of physicians. It was not until 1981 that the American Medical Association concluded that a patient has the right of self-determination; in order to exercise that right, the patient must have "enough information" to make an intelligent choice. Today, informed consent is firmly established as part of the law of negligence. There are both judicial and legislative rules that attempt to define the duties of physicians and the circumstances under which physicians will be liable for malpractice for failure to fulfill those duties (Katz).

The law's vision consists of shared decision-making. The doctor brings to the patient medical knowledge and judgment; the patient brings personal values. The law imposes on the doctor the duty of providing information, thus equalizing the relationship and enabling the patient to exercise judgment intelligently and rationally. The patient is to be sufficiently empowered so as to become an autonomous participant. The physician and patient share information and patiently explore alternatives; they share the burdens of decision. While they are bonded in their joint interests, they respect each other's autonomy.

In actual practice, very little shared decision-making occurs; instead, there is only disclosure of risk. The physician's goal is to get the patient to sign the consent form in order to protect the physician from malpractice. What the patient learns is typically derived from bits of information produced by the efforts of the doctors and nurses to obtain compliance and from "situational etiquette." Patients do not make decisions; they acquiesce in recommendations made by doctors (Lidz and Meisel 1982). Katz describes the dialogue as largely monologue: "[W]hat passes today for disclosure and consent ... is largely an unwitting attempt by physicians to shape the disclosure process so that patients will comply with their recommendations" (Katz:22, 26).

The written, signed consent form—the ultimate symbol of legal rationality—is the ultimate distortion. Neither the physicians nor the nurses view the form as part of the decision-making process; rather, it is a bureaucratic obstacle imposed upon them by hospital administrators and lawyers. In most cases, it is a preprinted form with minimal information. Patients, in effect, are asked to sign the forms *after* decisions are made. When surgery is to be performed, the form is presented the night before the scheduled operation. Nurses are responsible for obtaining the signature but they do not consider themselves responsible for providing information.

There are variations on this process. Some doctors disclose more than others; some engage in dialogue. There is also variation in terms of procedures. But, by and large, the general picture is one of failure. Instead of client self-determination or dialogue, there is domination. The relationship, in most situations, is *legal-bureaucratic* rather than *participatory*.

There are three principal reasons for the failure of the law's vision: the attitudes of physicians, the attitudes of patients, and the nature of the medical decision-making process. As stated, the paternalistic attitude of physicians fulfills deep-seated professional and psychological needs (Stone 1979). The attitudes and behaviors of the patients reinforce, or appear to reinforce, the belief systems. Medical knowledge is uncertain, and this fact imposes great burdens on professionals who have been trained to believe that they must make important decisions rapidly and confidently. Diagnosis typically involves rapid formulation, often on a preconscious level, of a series of conclusions and preferable alternatives; it is a temporal process. Physicians rarely see alternative possibilities; rather, for each problem there exists a medically preferred course of action. The issue for the doctor, then, is not shared decision-making but the problem of persuading the patient to accept proper treatment. By the time the physician is conversing with the patient, "The decision has been made—by the doctor. It is now, in the medical view, time to make a recommendation to the patient" (Lidz and Meisel:400).

Participatory Decision-making in the Treatment of
Chronically Ill Patients

An important exception to the above pattern occurs in the treatment of the chronically ill; in this situation, the physician-patient relationship is markedly different. These patients are given more information than acute care patients, they develop a better understanding of their conditions, and they assume a greater role in therapy decisions. Conversations between patients and doctors take place over an extended period of time, and, with the passage of time, there is increased understanding (Lidz and Meisel).

Most likely the clearest example of the dialogue between the physician and the patient involves cases relating to renal dialysis. In a study by Lidz and Meisel, patients faced with such treatment plans became very knowledgeable; they were active in their treatment; and "physicians spoke to them more casually, like old friends, and information presented at bedside rounds was often in the form of a conversation with the patient rather than the sotto voce shop talk between the doctors as occurred with so many other patient groups. In fact, the patients often spoke the same jargon as physicians and not infrequently diagnosed their own problems" (Lidz and Meisel:349–350). The study gave examples of the gradual, long-term learning process, wherein patients assumed an active role in the process; physicians seemed to rely on the patient's own observations; and patients had the knowledge, expressed their preferences, and were listened to in "tough situations."

Lidz and Meisel argue that the unique relationship of chronic patients is not primarily due to the experience of the patient in the patient role but to the demands placed on the patient by having a chronic disease. With chronic renal failure, patients are faced with lifetime restrictions and, unless they receive a transplant, dependence on a machine. In contrast with acute care patients, new renal failure patients are inundated with information as a genuine effort is made to inform them. Acknowledging that there are many reasons for giving information, the authors argue that the main reason is the nature of the treatment:

Patients on dialysis need to understand their disease and treatment because they need to cooperate much more actively than other patients. Not only are demands quantitatively greater (e.g., fluid and dietary restrictions) but also qualitatively greater. Renal patients . . . are encouraged to learn to run the dialysis machines themselves with the hope that many of them will eventually dialyze at home. To dialyze at home requires a great deal of knowledge. Family members are also frequently included because they serve as backups for home treatment. (Lidz and Meisel:352–353)

Renal patients are encouraged to learn about alternative treatments and are given real choices. They get to know other patients on the machines. "In observing the manner in which these patients were dealt with compared to the more 'cut and dried' acute cases, one gets the notion that these patients have been elected to a very select club. Suddenly they are treated more like equals in the treatment and decision-making processes" (Lidz and Meisel:353).

It is important to emphasize, as the authors do, that the physician–renal dialysis patient relationship was not based on the personality of the patient—what the patient necessarily *brought* to the therapeutic relationship; the authors found that when the renal dialysis patients became acute care patients, the traditional paternalistic relationship reasserted itself. In other words, the dialogue in the renal dialysis situation was created by the participants for the *particular situation*; shared decision-making was not something that the participants were necessarily predisposed to.

What accounts for the difference in the physician-patient relationship with the chronically ill? The difference lies in the professional task. The task of the surgeon is to perform a successful operation; informed consent is a legally imposed obstacle that must be negotiated. As long as a threshold of (legal) voluntariness has been reached, the reasons for the consent are not of great concern to the surgeon. In the case of the renal dialysis patient, the doctor's professional task is to assist the patient in learning to cope with a new way of life and taking the therapy. Here, the psychological needs and reasons of the patient are important. As distinguished from the surgeon's duties and interactions, passive cooperation is not enough: there also must be *understanding*; there must be patient explanation, extended conversations, and persuasion, the genuine sharing of information, and the empowerment of patients. The patients have to trust the physicians, but it is not the blind trust that the traditional physician engenders. Rather, it is trust based on understanding and confidence.

I must emphasize here the importance of the *reciprocal concrete incentives* to the process of participation. What accounts for the difference in the professional-patient relation for the surgeon as opposed to the renal dialysis physician? Both physicians are instrumental, but whereas in the case of the surgeon the instrumental task serves to distort the conversation, in the case of the renal dialysis physician genuine shared decision-making is *essential* to instrumentalism; otherwise, the doctor will fail in the task of stabilizing the patient. The authors of the study make the careful point that knowledge is not given to the renal dialysis patients "so they could be active decisionmakers per se, but so that they could be active treaters" (Lidz and Meisel:354). In the case of the surgeon, ethics and policy ask for shared decision-making, but shared decision-making is overwhelmed (colonized) by the demands of professionalism and the legal system; in the case of the renal dialysis physician, the demands of professionalism *require* shared decision-making. In the case of the surgeon, the material, social, and structural conditions of the relationship serve as barriers to communication; in the case of the renal dialysis physician, these same conditions *provide* the incentives for communication.

No one denies the importance of material, social, and structural conditions in preventing shared decision-making. What the relationship with the chronically ill shows is the possibility that these conditions may provide an *incentive* to engage in conversation.

Special Education

The Education for All Handicapped Children Act (P.L.94–142) was enacted in 1972 and was part of the vast changes in our legal system that established rights for minorities, the poor, women, the elderly, the mentally ill, and the handicapped. It was claimed that many handicapped children had been excluded from schools altogether and that those who were admitted were not given an adequate education; for the most part, they were improperly classified and segregated into tracts where self-fulfilling prophecies wasted their lives. Boys and minorities especially suffered.

P.L.94–142 gave all handicapped children the right to an "appropriate" public education but did not purport to define content. Specific, individual educational programs were to be decided by the relevant participants. School people would be the key decision-makers, but they were required to use multidisciplinary sources. The key institutional innovation, reflecting the spirit of the times, was the required participation of the parents. Parents of handicapped children had to be notified and give written consent before a child was to be selected for diagnosis, evaluated, and placed in a special education program. Evaluation had to be done by a multidisciplinary team; there was a conference in which the parent was entitled to be present. The parent who disagreed with any decision had a right to two administrative appeals (district and state) and judicial review. In sum the law set the framework for discussion and specified the relevant participants, but left it to the associated individuals to decide the concrete situation.

On some important levels, P.L.94–142 has been a success. A great deal of money is now spent on special education, handicapped children are admitted to public schools, and there are a lot of programs (Clune and Van Pelt 1985). What is not so clear is whether what is happening substantively in the classroom is that successful (Heller, Holtzman, and Messick 1982). But, in any event, there seems little doubt that the procedures designed to give the parents a participatory role in decisions affecting their children do not work.

Initially, school districts were decidedly cool to the new law; they were used to handling problem children their own way. With the law's passage, they had to follow complicated and cumbersome procedures involving conferences, multidisciplinary consultations, parental involvement, and burdensome paper work. Over time, the bureaucracy adjusted. Special education turned out to be a good program for schools: there were more resources; and special education slots were available to relieve regular teachers of troublesome children. Substantively, there was a shift away from a single psychologist, who administered an intelligence test, to a multi-team assessment, as required by law, but generally decisions were still made by one or two staff members. The most important information was academic performance, the students' behavioral or social needs, and the availability of slots. Despite the intent of the law, IQ tests still figured prominently. Once a student was placed, there were strong incentives to remain in that slot; most funding arrangements with local school districts were based on reimbursement for slots that were filled, and changes would entail substantially more paper work (Handler 1986; Heller, Holtzman, and Messick).

The procedures were also distorted by the exigencies of the bureaucracy. The average parent, especially one from a lower socioeconomic class, does not have the ability to participate. In addition to the psychological burdens of coping with a handicapped child, the parent lacks the information and the resources to deal with the school bureaucracy. Both participation in the meetings and the consent forms are usually formalities only. School districts decide the cases beforehand (in a process called "organizing the data"), consent forms are often signed before the placement meetings, and parents are usually presented with staff recommendations followed by ritualistic certification. Parents are outnumbered: they are strangers confronting a group of people who have worked together and struck a bargain; the discussion is often in technical jargon, often with the subtle implication that the child or the parent or both are at fault. In large districts, committees spend an average of two and a half minutes per decision.

This pattern varies according to the social class of the parents. The articulate, knowledgeable, middle- and upper-middle-class parents who press for expensive out-of-school placements for their severely handicapped children hold their own. But for the average lower-class or minority parents, their participation is ritualistic only;

they are silenced by administrative domination (Handler 1986; Heller et al.).

Toward Meaningful Participation: The Madison Example

The Madison, Wisconsin, school district operates differently. For historical reasons, prior to and without regard to the procedural requirements of P.L.94–142, the district made three conceptual moves that resulted in a vastly different client-agency relationship. The first change was to make parents part of the *solution* to special education rather than the problem. In order for special education to succeed, to prepare children for life in the non-school world as well as in school, parents were required to get involved in the education of their handicapped children; the school could not do it alone. This meant that parents had to understand and actively cooperate with both the in-school and out-of-school program. The second change implemented was a frank and genuine acknowledgment that, for most of those labeled mildly retarded, the technology was uncertain; diagnosis and treatment had to be flexible and experimental. This move lowered the level of potential conflict. As long as the two parties genuinely believed in experimentation, then one could comfortably concede the views of the other with the confidence that the matter was still open for renegotiation.

But what about resources? How were parents *able* to participate, to become part of the solution? For these questions the district conceived of the third change, a *parent advocate*—a lay person who was experienced in the process (usually a parent of a handicapped child)—to help the newly involved parent. In contrast to most communitarian-oriented plans—where conflict is viewed negatively—conflict was deliberately introduced to aid communication; it was not *adversarial* conflict, but *communicative* conflict. As teachers and school psychologists reported, the parent advocates would ask questions in the meetings that the parents were afraid to ask or did not know how to ask.

The deliberate introduction of conflict as a necessity for communication is an example of a genuine commitment to shared decision-making. A genuine dialogue entails mutual respect, sincere listening, an openness to test opinions. The school people did not want the parents to abdicate to experts. It was through the give-and-take and conversation that consensus and generalized interests would be discovered. The school staff acknowledged the uncertainty of the technology, and they wanted the parents to feel comfortable with the decisions. The decisions were experimental and flexible; although hunches, intuitions, and guesses all played a role, the process was fundamentally rational—ultimately, the participants had the obligation to support their positions with the best possible reasons and arguments.

Other key factors that were necessary in making the Madison approach succeed included, for example, social movement activities such as parent groups, training sessions, and so forth. Parents had to have access to their own experts who could participate in the conferences and to school people willing to listen to outside opinions.

Although I did not complete a full-scale empirical examination of the Madison system, there was strong evidence that it contained a distinctly different system of parent-teacher interactions. It was far from perfect and significant weaknesses appeared, but the system also was not a sham (Handler 1986).

In both special education and informed consent in medicine, we are presented with regulatory failures. In both cases, attempts were made to alter relationships by changing the procedures. But changes in procedures were not enough. The issue of power was not addressed, and in both domains, dependent people were not able to participate. The incentives of the bureaucracy were able to distort and ultimately nullify the liberal legal procedural changes. In both situations, as far as the powerless were concerned, there was monologue, not dialogue.

Something more is required to restrain the power of the legal, economic, or administrative systems from distorting personal interactions. In the Madison School system, as with the renal dialysis relationship, *reciprocal concrete incentives* were changed. The Madison school district and the renal dialysis physician decided that in order to accomplish their tasks, they had to get the understanding and cooperation of the parents and the patients; but it was not simple cooperation—all school districts and surgeons are legally required to obtain that—they had to get the *active* cooperation of the participants. To achieve active cooperation, there must be understanding, persuasion, and reciprocity.

Community-Based Care for the Frail, Elderly Poor

The situation of elderly patients in nursing homes is perhaps an extreme example of regulatory failure. The core of the relationship—the quality of the interaction between the resident and the staff—is, for the most part, beyond regulation. Regulation is forced to monitor inputs—fire and safety, nutrition, staffing ratios and credentials, records, and so forth—in terms of minimum standards. Codes are large, complex, and detailed. Because residents are so dependent and usually so frail, regulation has the heavy burden of generating all of its information. Because there is a shortage of beds and the potential of harm during patient transfer, it is difficult to impose meaningful sanctions. Today, life in most nursing homes is relatively safe; serious fires and food poisoning, for example, are rare. On the other hand, life there is probably unhealthy and certainly boring (Vladeck). Residents of nursing homes are among our most vulnerable populations; even prisoners can riot.

How would it be possible to attain shared decision-making in this situation? The community of residents in a particular nursing home does not have to be taken as given. If we compare the health and functional status of elderly persons of similar age groups, we find that there is not a great difference between most nursing-home residents and people living in the community in terms of health and disability. The key difference between the two groups is that those living in the community have someone to take care of them—usually either a spouse or an adult child (frequently a daughter). These "informal care-givers" provide a great deal of care; in contrast, the residents of nursing homes are on their own (E. Abel 1987). For historical reasons, we decided to follow a medical model to take care of the frail elderly in nursing homes. These elderly people become alone and then are segregated into hospital-like institutions (Vladeck).

If we think of the population in terms of the numbers of aging individuals, we see a continuum: some are quite healthy and independent; others vary in degree of disability and health status and in terms of informal care; and some are very ill and disabled, and quite close to death. Many elderly live alone, or with their spouses, or with or near their children and do quite well, or at least well enough so as not to require institutional care. Most of the elderly who need help receive "informal" help from relatives and friends. In many communities, there are formal programs of community care such as adult day care, respite, home health aides, chore services, and the like. But there are, too, those elderly who become alone, very disabled, and need an extensive amount of custodial care (E. Abel).

A variety of publicly funded programs have been designed to encourage the informal care system. There are a variety of motives behind the programs—people want to avoid nursing homes, they receive better care in the community, and so forth—but a principal motive is to save public funds. Nursing homes are a huge drain on public funds (Medicaid) and it is thought that keeping the elderly in the community longer will be expensive.

As it turns out, not surprisingly, informal care in the community is not necessarily cheaper than the average cost of nursing-home care under Medicaid. Medicaid reimbursement rates have been held down for several years; community care can be expensive. In addition, it is difficult to restrict enrollment to people who have potential informal care-givers *and* who, but for the additional help, would go to a nursing home. In many programs, it turned out that the additional help was just that and not a substitute for the nursing home. Thus, there was no saving of public funds (Weissert 1985).

Community-based care for the frail, elderly poor is an example of public policy, law, and administration trying to preserve, maintain, and enhance relationships of the most intimate, sensitive, and fragile kind. The paradigmatic example is the adult daughter or elderly spouse, who are often not in the best of health, taking care of the disabled patient. Along with caring activities, there is often great psychological, social, and financial stress (E. Abel).

How does law and administration intervene to preserve and enhance this relationship? The regulatory challenges are daunting. The client population is hard to reach; the frail, alone elderly are notorious for their often self-defeating independence; and when reached, they are passive and accepting rather than complainers or rights-bearing citizens. They are easily frightened and manipulated by aggressive and unscrupulous vendors. The quality of the product that is delivered is difficult to observe and measure. Distribution, for most services, is in the home. How helpful and kind was the home help aide? How long did the physical therapist, in fact, stay, and what kind and how good was the therapy that was given? Is the transportation service patient and supportive or indifferent, rushed, and abrupt? The style and attitudes of the services are important if they are not to become barriers and contributors to additional anxieties, depressions, and other forms of disability. In nursing homes, the state regulatory agencies have to generate all the relevant information, and, as a result, regulation has become oppressive, clumsy, ineffective, and distorting. Given the nature of the services and the characteristics of the clients, accountability is a serious concern, but how can there be effective accountability in community-based care without intrusive, distorting regulation?

Meaningful Participation in Community-Based Care for the Frail Elderly

I examined several voluntary and for-profit agencies in the Los Angeles area that are operating community care programs for the frail, elderly poor. First I will discuss the voluntary agencies, and then the for-profits.[9]

There are a variety of programs within each voluntary agency, but, essentially, the agencies recruit eligibles, provide case management, and contract services from other agencies according to the needs of each client. Quite often, case management consists of working with the informal care-givers, usually the adult children, in helping them to work in various ways with their disabled parent. Most help is aimed at the routine, mundane tasks ("assistance in daily

---

9. Three voluntary and five for-profit agencies were selected. The agencies were purposively selected on the basis of community reputation for administering exemplary programs. They are not representative. My purpose was to determine whether client empowerment and dialogism could occur in real-life situations.

living") such as cleaning, nutrition, bathing, toileting, and transporting—activities which, if not done, will result in serious, rapid deterioration to the point that the client requires institutionalization.

The service most often contracted for is home help, which, in addition to the specific chores, also provides crucial respite for the informal care-givers. Many other services are also provided—therapy, adult day care, transportation, chore services, and health care.

While there are many interesting aspects to this program, I emphasize here how law and administration operate to provide a framework for shared decision-making. As with our prior examples, the focus is on the reciprocal concrete incentives. I found that, in order for the agencies to establish and maintain an effective care system, they had to enlist the active cooperation of the participants and, if available, of their informal care-givers. While there are important caring benefits from such an arrangement, it is important to recognize the several tangible, concrete benefits to the agency.

One of the requirements of the Medicaid waiver is that the agency cannot spend, on average, more than ninety-five percent of the cost the participant would pay in a Medicaid nursing home. This is an important financial constraint because the agency cannot come in under the cost constraint without the active participation of the client and the informal care-givers; they have to share the work. In order to obtain that active participation, the family must understand and agree with the agency plan: they must work together. For example, if a home aide is needed, the agency must work with the client and/or the adult daughter and train them to interview, select, monitor, and, if necessary, discharge a county-supplied home help aide. If the agency has to do all of these activities, it becomes too expensive administratively; if they are not done, the client does not receive good home help. The agency also must have similarly cooperative relationships in terms of community-based programs such as transportation, adult day care, recreation, health care, and so forth. In the agency jargon, the client and/or the informal care-givers have to become "ad hoc case managers."

One important consequence of these cooperative client relationships is the impact on the regulatory task. To the extent that informal care-givers are involved, information is generated by the clients. Not only is more information generated (there is, in effect, continual on-site inspection), but a different quality is generated as well: we now have personal reports of quality of care rather than an inspector who relies on records and interviews. Compare a familiar example—a cooperative day care arrangement where parents share teaching responsibilities with the staff. The participating parents have personal quality assurance information. The three voluntary agencies I studied rely extensively on client-generated information.

From the perspective of the staff and the voluntary agencies, there were three structural reasons or incentives for client participation. First, there were professional norms. The agency and the staff believed in client empowerment; clients could take more control over their lives and they would be better off. Second, the technological processes encouraged participation; the clients (and the informals), in effect, shared the work *and* provided valuable information. This greatly lessened the regulatory monitoring burdens on the agencies and, thus, the clients had a valuable resource that the agency needed. Third was the financial constraint: the agencies could not do all of the work and stay within the financial cap. Again, this meant that the clients had a valuable resource.[10]

The For-Profit Agencies

In the three voluntary agencies, the norms of participation were reinforced by complementary concrete incentives. What would the incentives be in for-profit agencies? If the program has the same professional ideologies as the voluntary agencies, and has a similar structure, then the client-agency relationship should be approximately the same. If the program pays per unit of service, then providers would stay as long as possible, do as much as possible, and the clients would remain passive. If the program is tightly limited per unit of service (e.g., Medicare home help), then the clients will be involved, but in a passive, instrumental manner rather than in joint decision-making. In other words, consistent with existing re-

---

10. Two of the agencies had a fourth structural variable. One agency was strongly rooted in the community; there were extensive personal relationships among staff, volunteers, and clients. The other agency structured community participation in many parts of governance, including the important grievance committee.

search, it is not the form of ownership that matters as much as the structure of the program (Kramer 1987).

For-profit agencies are reimbursed either through Medicare or private pay (out-of-pocket or insurance). Medicare covers short-term, intermittent care in the home—nursing, physical therapy, occupational therapy, speech therapy, and home health aides; it does not cover homemakers. The home health aide is limited to hourly visits and can only be in the home if there is another primary discipline providing services (e.g., nursing, physical therapy). Medicare services are highly regulated and strictly limited to only that which is necessary to take care of the medical problem. Private pay offers whatever range of services is contracted for. In the agencies studied, the range went from homemaker to live-ins (some have stayed as long as five years). Some programs include case management.

In all, five agencies were researched. One of the agencies—part of a national chain—which administered a privately financed program, took an "hours and sales" approach; lengthy care was viewed as a benefit to the agency; client education and independence were not encouraged. The client was the "patient"; the customer—the one who paid the bill—played a larger role in decision-making. But this agency was at one end of the spectrum.

All of the other agencies adopted and practiced, in varying degrees, what they called "client empowerment strategies." They considered clients as part of the decision-making process and valued client independence. Family involvement was encouraged. All of the agencies, whether private pay or Medicare, developed care plans. The service coordinator screened the client and made initial determinations. A nurse made the home visit for the initial assessment. Clinical supervisors (registered nurses) made periodic visits for quality assurance. In most of the agencies, there was some form of case management; in three, the staff advocated on behalf of clients with insurance companies. The staff coordinator or case manager monitored the service providers.

In Medicare, strict regulations and paper requirements limited sharing, although clients did participate in the scheduling of services. On the other hand, Medicare does encourage client education. With the exception of the one private pay agency, which treated the family as the customer, all of the other agencies encouraged family involvement. Several had the family become involved in the initial planning sessions. The agencies strongly encouraged family involvement because of the strict program limits; the client and the family had to take over the care.

In the private-pay programs, there was more direct client supervision of the providers. With the one exception, all of the agencies stressed the importance of trust and empowerment. They all stressed independence, shared decision-making, and dignity as goals that were important in both their own right as well as in the therapeutic benefits they engendered. One example of independence involved a client homebound because of incontinence. Home health services can provide an aide to put in a catheter three times a week; but the agency preferred to train the client (or the family) in order to maintain her independence. Other education programs involved diet and medication. This was the general pattern of the agencies, although commitment to empowerment, strategies, and results varied among staff and clients.

One of the for-profit agencies is a hospital that runs a program similar to the voluntary agency programs; it uses multidisciplinary case management and the range of services, but also includes a more extensive package of health care and social services. In addition to social workers, the agency teams include gerontologically trained internists and psychiatrists. The program is modeled after the British day hospital. The hospital's geriatric program is quite similar to the voluntary agencies—focusing on multidisciplinary, holistic assessments; joint participation in the development and administration of the care plan; and extensive reliance on client information, supervision, and complaints. Family involvement is emphasized. The dominating professional norm is "functional independence" rather than the "invalid role," despite the fact that this program is run out of a hospital.

Why is the hospital's geriatric program (apparently) successful? I found structural patterns similar to the voluntary agencies. The professional norms within the program have been changed from the medical model; gerontologically trained physicians favor for therapeutic reasons the holistic, empowering approach. As with the voluntary agency programs, the technology encouraged client (and family) involvement, including the all-important information and monitoring functions. There were also strong economic reasons for the program's success: the geriatric program operates at a loss, but it is supported by the hospital as a method of recruiting geriatric patients. As with all of the programs discussed, there is complementarity between professional norms, technology, and economics.

In these examples of community-based care, the clients and the informal care-givers become part of the solution. Instead of being mere recipients of services on a take-it-or-leave-it basis, their active participation in the program is a requirement for the agencies; they provide crucial services and crucial information without which the agencies could not succeed.

To the extent that the agencies are successful in involving family as part of the solution, we are observing client-agency relationships that have elements similar to the Madison school district and the renal dialysis relationship. The relationships have a strong instrumental base—we begin with reciprocal concrete incentives—but there also has to be reciprocal *trust*: we find this trust throughout the case manager and client interviews. Careful, patient, one-on-one conversations take place; clients and family are slowly brought into the program; confidences are established between the client, the family, and the staff; and they begin to rely on each other for their most intimate needs. As in the examples of the teachers and the renal dialysis physician, the professional task is defined in terms of cooperation based on understanding and trust.

In order for this kind of participation to occur, a great deal of trust among all of the participants was required. Clients would not have participated, accepted services, shared the work, and reported honestly and accurately unless they believed in the competence and good faith of the agency and the staff. The case managers, too, had to trust the clients: clients were given large responsibilities and unless there were both understanding and capacity, client cooperation would be unreliable; the case managers believed in the autonomy and responsibility of the clients. Thus, the professional staff role was redefined in two ways: reciprocal concrete incentives flowed back and forth between the professionals and the clients—there was a partnership—and their relationship was founded on trust.

What happens now with the nursing-home resident? The ideal scenario would involve a radical change in the way the more severely disabled elderly are cared for. Many commentators have called for different kinds of custodial and institutional care arrangements in which the residents are not radically separated from the community. In certain retirement communities, for example, extensive amounts of health and health-related custodial care are given on the premises; the residents remain in their communities with their friends and relatives. But those kinds of arrangements, unfortunately, are primarily restricted to the wealthy few: in today's existing nursing-home structure most of the frail, poor elderly will die either in hospitals or in hospital-like nursing homes.

I believe, however, that when certain participants of the community-based care programs that I have described eventually need to go to a nursing home, they may be going under different circumstances. Their informal care-givers have now been trained and socialized into dealing with agencies: they know how to get information, and they have contacts within the agencies they have been dealing with if they need advice and help; they are much more informed. The networks that have been built up in the community-based program could penetrate the walls of the nursing home and could continue. Again, there are important concrete benefits to the regulatory agencies and the nursing homes that are interested in quality of care as well as administrative compliance. There is now an important source of reliable information. Unfortunately, the programs that I am studying terminate when the participant enters a nursing home, so the agencies cannot really engage in extensive follow-up; however, the agencies have been reporting that on occasion, informally, what I have predicted has happened, at least for short periods of time.

This is not entirely utopian speculation. There have been several demonstration projects wherein families and volunteers have become actively involved with nursing-home residents. There is an exchange of useful information, and the more the mutual trust, the better the information. New federal nursing-home legislation and regulations emphasize access and organization by family members, friends, and organizations. This reflects the strong view of the Institute of Medicine as well as other commentators that the presence of outsiders is crucial to the key goal of improving the relationship between the aide and the resident so that residents are treated in a pleasant, interesting, respectful, and autonomous manner: one that is helpful, dignified, and caring (Institute of Medicine; Vladeck).

Studies have shown that residents benefit and the quality of the home is likely to be higher when there is community involvement. The frequent presence of visitors encourages staff attention to both residents and their roommates. Community groups provide outside contact; they mediate disputes and monitor care. Support groups exchange information and discuss strategies, including advocacy (E. Abel; Butler 1980). Vladeck argues that regulation can strengthen community ties through mandated boards of visitors and/or required volunteer programs; several states have such programs (Vladeck). The nursing home literature also discusses examples of homes and staffs that have benefited from community involvement (Butler; Doty and Sullivan 1983). Family, friends, and volunteers can supplement care. This research shows that frail, elderly people, whether in nursing homes or in the community, need strong structural and professional support if they are to become empowered.

What Type of Community?

In the three examples discussed above, the story of the dominant legal-bureaucratic regime is familiar—the failure of liberal legal due process to protect the powerless; the role of law, bureaucracy, and politics in the steady growth of command-and-control regulation; and the jurisprudential critique of liberal legalism.

But what accounts for the participatory exceptions? In discussing the exceptions, I pointed to three structural variables: professional norms, the technology of the work (shared tasks), and the financial incentives. In all of these examples, there were good intentions (professional norms), but there was also something more—there were reciprocal concrete incentives. These incentives were necessary, I believe, not only to get the conversation started, but also to keep it going; otherwise, the pressures would become too great and gradually, insidiously, undermine the conversation.

Participation may become ritualistic only: there are numerous examples where this occurs. In the early days of Legal Services, idealistic poverty lawyers struggled to establish and maintain dialogue with their clients, but became overwhelmed by the work load, bureaucratic requirements, and client dependency (Wexler 1970). Social workers frequently complain about the difficulty of maintaining empowerment relationships in the bureaucratic setting. The pressures in the contemporary organization of medicine limit the "caring functions" of health care. In the Madison school district, the teachers struggle to maintain the active involvement of the parents as well as their own willingness to genuinely listen. Genuine listening is a difficult art. In the participatory examples, there are important instrumental reasons for the professional to listen; otherwise, she cannot perform her task.

Reciprocal incentives, then, can produce cooperation, but not necessarily dialogism. They can be strictly instrumental. Dialogism is a moral position; instrumental relations can be morally indifferent. Dialogism can be instrumental, but it is also something more. What I argue is that the kinds of concrete reciprocal incentives that are involved in the three participatory examples—understanding *and* active cooperation—are the kinds of moral values that the communitarian feminists and the modern/postmodern dialogical philosophers are talking about. In those examples, the moral values are the *preconditions* of instrumentalism.

Baier's analysis of trust helps distinguish dialogism from cooperation. In the study of the renal dialysis patients, there were strong mutual reciprocal incentives built around the treatment: the patients want to be stabilized, and physicians want to perform their professional tasks. I have called this concept "reciprocal concrete incentives"; Baier refers to this as a common good or as professional pride in the competent discharge of responsibilities. There are strong psychological elements involved in pursuing the common good. The patient has to assume large responsibilities for her welfare in order for there to be a successful treatment; *passive* acceptance of doctor's orders is not satisfactory. The patient has to have confidence in the professional competence and goodwill of the physician and in the idea that the physician does have the patient's best interest at heart. The physician is relying on the intelligence and judgment of the patient to absorb the information, to use it properly, and to make intelligent decisions. Both realize that there are important quality-of-life considerations and that both are equal moral agents. Trust is based on a rational assessment of goodwill, respect, and autonomy. Trust, thus, not only survives Baier's test of expressibility, but grows stronger.

It would seem that Baier's test also applies to the Madison special education example. In the Madison system, as in any complex interaction, there are a lot of instrumental exchanges—primarily of information, but also in the sharing of routine tasks, meetings, and so forth—but the foundation is basic, reciprocal trust. There has to be reciprocal trust for the system to work. Consider the following quote from a lower-class, not well-educated parent: "Our family has never been criticized, they've never said, 'You're failing him.' They've encouraged us to allow him to do more and try more, and not to be afraid. They've convinced us he can do more than we think he can do" (Handler 1986:79). The school must get the parent involved, to push the child, to get the child to do more; this is accomplished through out-of-school activities (a basic innovation in the Madison system). The school would not pursue this course unless it believed in the parent and had confidence in what the parent understood and could do. When the parent was passive and hesitant, the school had to *convince* the parent to let the child do more than the parent thought the child could do. The parent would not have done so unless she understood and trusted the school staff. To gain that trust, the school workers did not criticize the parent, they did not put her down, they did not seek domination. Instead, they sought and obtained understanding, trust, and cooperation. The school did not order the parent on pain of sanction: they talked to her, they persuaded her, they convinced her.

Other empirical examples rose out of the Madison school district program. Plans were tentative, always subject to renegotiation. If parents did not feel comfortable with a particular recommendation, the school would try another on an experimental basis. This kind of negotiation and flexibility on the part of the school and the parents also required both understanding and reciprocal trust. It also involved practical judgment. There were occasions when parents simply did not feel comfortable with the recommendations; but feelings and intuitions were important, because trust and cooperation were necessary. At times, parents would become passive and teachers would insist on more active participation (e.g., requiring parents to complete the reports and recommendations); the teachers needed active, understanding parents. The conversation had to continue during the school life of the child. In other words, the moral values of the communitarian feminists and the dialogical philosophers were those that were necessary to make reciprocity work in this context. The school system needed cooperation based on understanding.

We also find similar relationships in the community-based care of the frail, elderly poor. There is dependency on the part of the clients; there is the giving of concrete services; and there are the instrumental, organizational, and staff incentives on the part of the agencies. Nevertheless, this still seems to be a case of a morally decent trust. In many of the cases, the agency had to persuade the elderly people to become involved, to sign on. These are poor, dependent people; they are living on the edge, both financially and physically; many are not willing or able psychologically to become involved in a strange, new relationship. The reluctance of old people to participate in social programs is well documented. Involving their adult children is also often not an easy task. There may be complicated historical relationships to work out, as well as the reluctance of parents to ask children for help. In any event, we have heard repeated stories from the staff as to how they often have to work quite slowly, patiently building up confidences, and making sure they understand the client's needs and anxieties. There are times when the staff got ahead of the client and wanted to do things for the client that the client was not ready for; they were simple tasks that seemed obviously beneficial (such as cleaning the apartment), but in the context, they posed threats and created anxieties for these very dependent people. Services worked best when there was trust, when the clients came to believe in the goodwill of the staff, and when there was joint participation.

The elderly patients are not only needed as clients for the program, they also perform active services for the staff. They must participate in hiring and supervising service providers; they must report information; and they must call in at frequent intervals to maintain appropriate contact. These reciprocal tasks would not be undertaken in this manner unless there was mutual confidence in the abilities and judgment on the part of both staff and client. They would not survive unless reciprocity was based on goodwill and professional pride; thus, the test of expressibility is satisfied.

These examples are three instances of morally decent trust relationships. In all three, there was a considerable imbalance of power; yet, in all three, the dependent participants were equal moral agents. Trust altered the power relationships. The relationships thrived on trust based on goodwill. If the instrumental community is amoral, in the sense of being unconcerned with motives, and the dialogical community is moral, then these seem to be examples of purposive dialogism, the active seeking of reciprocal moral bonds. One of the distinctions that Baier draws between contracts and trust involves the state of mind of the participants:

[C]ontracts themselves do not express what it is in the state of mind of the other that each party relies on to get what he wants from the deal.... It is not part of contracts or social contracts to specify what assumptions each party needs to make about the other in respect of such psychological factors [as] love, fear, ignorance, sense of powerlessness, good nature, inattention, which one can use for one's secret purposes. (Baier:257)

It is precisely the psychological factors of goodwill, professional pride, altruism, and respect which make the relationships with the renal dialysis patient, the parent, and the frail, elderly poor thrive.

How does Baier's test apply to apparently more instrumental relationships—for example, Hawkins's water pollution inspectors? It will be recalled that the inspectors engaged in a cooperative style of regulation with the industry. Forbearance or enforcement depended on judgments of blameworthiness; sanctions would be imposed for intentional acts or an uncooperative attitude. There was an exchange of reciprocal benefits. The industry was relieved of suspicious, by-the-book regulation and sanctions for accidents. The agency could ration scarce resources, had easier access to property and information, and felt free to discuss sensitive issues. Not infrequently, there would be self-reporting. Corrective measures could be tailored to individual situations. The agency felt that regulatory goals were being met.

It is clear that there are large elements of trust in the relationship that Hawkins describes. The actors trust each other to abide by the rules in a manner similar to Axelrod's tit for tat. As Bardach and Kagan point out in their work, this is no small achievement. How would Baier's expressibility test apply to this relationship? What is the psychological position of the actors? It is the avoidance of the costs of strict enforcement that provides the basis for the cooperative style of regulation. Both the industry and the agency will achieve their goals at lower costs if they cooperate rather than become adversaries. But what kind of a trust is this? It is not a "morally rotten" trust in that exposure of the motives would destabilize the relationship. Would exposure of motives strengthen the trust? In the moral trust, exposure of mutual love, goodwill, altruism, and respect are common goods in themselves and would strengthen the moral trust. This is not necessarily the case with Hawkins's example. Exposure of the motives would strengthen the relationship if the costs of strict enforcement were thereby made more clear or new ones were exposed. Exposure would have no effect if there was not additional information. More significantly, the costs of strict enforcement are not *common goods:* each party has its own costs; each makes its own calculation. Cooperation is not the common good; cooperation is only the instrument for reducing the individual costs of doing business. And, if the individual costs for one of the parties exceed its individual benefits, the cooperation will end. The agency will do its job through strict enforcement; the industry will keep producing, and one of its costs will be resistance or compliance. As long as there is clarity and as long as the benefit/cost calculation works out, cooperation can be based on suspicion and fear as well as goodwill.

But how is this different from the renal dialysis example? There, it will be recalled, reciprocal activities were designed to improve treatment. Treatment is individualized—the patient is stabilized and the professional has performed the task. There are important differences between the renal dialysis relationship and the water pollution control relationship which suggest the differences between dialogism and instrumental cooperation. The differences concern power relationships, the psychological effects on the parties, and the nature of the common good. In the renal dialysis example, the relationship becomes constitutive and transformative in ways that do not apply to the water pollution control example.

Power has been altered in the case of the renal dialysis patient: the patient has been given information and responsibility; there has been an empowerment of a dependent person. Power, says Arendt, is created through participation; thus, in this very important sense, involving the very life of the patient, the relationship is transformative. This is not necessarily the case with the water pollution control example; indeed, the opposite is usually presumed, as it involves two relatively equal agents dealing with each other. As a result of the cooperation, both will be better off, and in that sense, there is change, but power has not necessarily been altered.

Additionally, in the renal dialysis case, the change is also constitutive, because the change in the social practices of the patient necessarily implies a change in the patient's ideologies. The change in power, the ability of the patient to take control of her life, means that there has been a change in the patient's self-conception and in the patient's views about the disease and her relationship with the physician and allied health professionals. Ideology is not separate from action, but it is integral to social practices. Ideology defines experiences and social relationships; it constructs reality (Merry).

We find the same constitutive and transformative change in ideologies and practices for the special education parent and the frail, elderly poor. It will be recalled that one parent acknowledged her change in self-conception and in her ideas about what she could now do with her child. The frail elderly poor also take more control over their lives. Empowerment in all three examples is both transformative and constitutive. Empowerment is not necessarily implied in instrumental cooperation. Neither the water pollution control inspector nor the factory owner have necessarily developed changed ideologies about themselves and their relationship.

In addition to separate, instrumental benefits there is also a common good in the three empirical examples. None of the relationships could survive without goodwill, altruism, and mutual respect; indeed, the relationships thrive because of the presence of goodwill. Applying Baier's test of expressibility, goodwill becomes an additional common good between the parties. In the parent of a special education child and the elderly poor examples, there were genuinely affectionate, respectful, altruistic statements made on both sides. In the water pollution control example, moral states of mind—respect, friendship, and so forth—are not precluded, but they are not crucial for the cooperative behavior; all that is needed is clarity, on both sides, as to the relative benefits and costs of alternative behavior. This is not the case with the three participatory examples. The treatment of the renal dialysis patient, the special education of the handicapped child, and the support for the frail, elderly poor could not be accomplished without the moral states of mind that Baier has identified. These moral states of mind become an additional common good. The relationships in the three participatory examples seem quite different from instrumental cooperation.

How Much Empowerment?

What do we mean by empowerment? How is power exercised in these relationships? Do the clients described in the participatory examples exercise power?

In Chapter 2, the various manifestations of power were described. At one level, the manifestation of power over clients in social service relationships is obvious. The client has to pay a price to receive the goods that the agent controls—usually a behavioral change in return for income or services. The client has a grievance, but lacks the ability to contest the decision.

Power is also exercised in more subtle ways (Lukes). In many instances, the powerless are excluded altogether from decision-making arenas; there are barriers to even expressing grievances. In welfare, for example, certain key decisions are decided legislatively and are not subject to the fair hearing process. In nursing-home regulation, the new law is designed to give residents a voice in areas where they have previously been excluded—for example, in regard to transfers and discharges.

There is yet another dimension of power—where grievances do not even become conscious. Consensus is manipulated: A exercises power over B by influencing, shaping, and determining B's very wants. The manifestation of power here looks to the social and historical contexts of the participants as well as to the subjective effects of politics in shaping demands and expectations (Edelman; Gaventa). As discussed in Chapter 2, quiescence not only comes about through the control of information and socialization processes, but also from the psychological adaptations of the powerless—fatalism, self-deprecation, apathy, and the internalization of dominant values and beliefs.

In social service relationships, power is exercised in all of its manifestations. Workers have multiple sources of power. They control the resources and services of the agency; they have expertise, persuasion, interpersonal skills, and legitimacy; they control information and the range of available alternatives; and they invoke the rules (Hasenfeld 1987). If the clients want the resources, they must yield at least some control over their lives. Power is not unrestrained; there are rules and regulations and professional norms. Nevertheless, in the case of vulnerable people, the relationship attained is largely involuntary since agencies are usually in a monopoly position.

I also outlined in Chapter 2 how the worker and the client bring to the social service exchange their respective social systems—who they are, what they represent, what they do, their characters, self-conceptions, and identities—which have been formed not only by their immediate lives but also by their past social relationships. The structures of their everyday lives affect their language, beliefs, and the symbols which shape their identities and direct their behavior. Ideologies, beliefs, and the social construction of reality have particular importance to the social service relationship. Social service agencies are designed to change people; hence, they are *moral* systems. As clients are recruited, processed, and evaluated, they are invested with moral and cultural qualities by the workers who select those clients; the clients serve the interests of the workers either by confirming their ideologies or conforming to the demands of their working conditions. By screening incompatible information, the workers' moral evaluations are confirmed through self-fulfilling prophecies (Hasenfeld 1987). A substantial amount of the literature shows evidence of dependent people internalizing the values and beliefs of the powerful or becoming apathetic (Bumiller; Felstiner, Abel, and Sarat). It is no wonder that dependent clients, and especially the frail, elderly poor, either fail to pursue or even conceptualize grievances; they develop a "culture of silence" (Freire).

If social work practice is viewed as the exchange of resources, clients are thus dependent if they lack resources that the agency needs. Power relations are altered by increasing client resources. Empowerment means the ability to control one's environment; thus, clients must have sufficient resources (including alternatives) to be able to make choices and to negotiate more favorable outcomes (Hasenfeld 1987). Client-worker practice has to shift from its individual orientation to a more structural approach to help people connect with needed resources. Client strategies include increasing information, improving personal skills, increasing collective strength, and improving links to alternatives. In the participatory examples, structural conditions were such that clients had resources—they were needed to share the work, they supplied valuable information, and they were necessary for the proper performance of the professional task.

While these empowerment strategies are primarily addressed to situations in which clients perceive grievances or conflicts and lack the resources to complain and negotiate, they may have deeper possibilities. I have argued that relationships based on morally decent trust are not only empowering in an instrumental sense, but also in their effect on self-conception, conception of others, and the relationship; there is a reconstruction of the social world of the clients and workers. In other words, structural changes may affect the cultural contexts of the participants. The destabilization of power relationships, structures, and roles will produce changes in ideologies and beliefs. The participants will view themselves and their relationship differently (Merry). In the participatory examples, in order for the workers to share responsibility with the clients, the workers must believe that the clients understand, agree, and are willing to cooperate; workers must respect the capabilities, autonomy, and responsibility of the clients. The clients, in turn, will not give this kind of response unless they have confidence in the workers' competence and professionalism, and believe that they share a common belief in the clients' best interests. For the dependent client, empowerment requires more than passive quiescence; it requires active, understanding participation, and this requires trust.

In traditional social services, the clients are invested with moral characteristics that serve the interests of the workers. Empowered clients are also invested with moral characteristics, but the interests of the workers differ from traditional social work practice. The redefined professional task puts trust at the center of the relationship—not blind trust (quiescence) or trust based on sanctions, for those kinds of trust will not work for empowerment, but morally decent trust, where the clients' confidence in themselves and in the case managers and mutual understanding are crucial. In contrast to traditional social services practices, the ascribed moral characteristics are empowering rather than subordinating. The clients are changed not only in terms of their relationships with the case managers but also in their self-conceptions.

Still, one must be cautious. These findings are based on stories told by staff and several clients and their families. The clients are sick, old, weak, alone, and poor; they are very dependent. And the case managers and other staff are middle-class professionals employed by powerful agencies. The clients are "success" cases in that they are on the program and have good relations with the staff; they minimize (if not forget) past problems and focus on the present. The staff is attuned to the current professional rhetoric. Thus, we might wonder how much of what is told is ideological construction. How much change has occurred?

Consider the contrast between the clients in the voluntary agencies and the Medicare clients in the for-profit agencies. The former were involved in the full range of decisions from the very beginning. The latter were excluded from most of the important decisions. The doctors diagnosed, treated, and prescribed the medical problem. The home health aide, under the close supervision of the health care professionals, *instructed* the client (patient) on how to administer health care during the tightly controlled time that the home service was provided. We would be tempted to say that there was much more empowerment with the voluntary agency client; the Medicare patient, after all, was only instrumentally trained to perform a mechanical task. But do we know this? It may be that for a frail, elderly person to self-administer an injection is an enormously empowering act. In view of the subtleties of the manifestations of power, we need similar kinds of conceptualizations and operational definitions of empowerment. In these selected case studies, we seem to see empowering activities, but there are serious theoretical and empirical pitfalls.

Communities for Dependent People: Transformative, Constitutive, Partial, and Transitory

We must also not exaggerate the changes that have been described—that dependent people seem to be listened to, that they have taken some control over some part of their lives, that there is a sharing of power, that there is equal moral agency based on trust. These changes are partial. One would hope that the skills and self-perceptions learned here would apply to other areas of their lives, but this is unknown. One would hope that the moral responsiveness of the staff would also be applied to dependent people in other relationships; this, too, is unknown.

Moreover, the relationships described here may also be transitory. Clients change in terms of health, disability, and social relationships, all of which can affect their beliefs and attitudes. Even in the relationships that have been described, the case managers often have to work constantly to maintain active, understanding participation. This should not be surprising; human relationships are dynamic (Rorty 1989:42) and this population is very dependent.

Other objections may be raised about my conception of community. In the examples that I gave, there was the conscious, deliberate *creation* of community. Although Sandel does not say this, he seems to imply that communities already exist (Sandel:152). Bernstein notes that the dialogians seem to have an incipient presupposition of community. Baier, too, emphasizes the natural growth of trust rather than its deliberate creation. While Baier emphasizes the importance of trust in noncontractual relations, it is difficult to understand the reasons or to accept the implications that communities are not amenable to deliberate creation. Perhaps there is a feeling of inconsistency between instrumentalism and the humanistic values of community. But, in any event, the conservative implications of this position are profound, and must be rejected. I return to Bernstein where he urges us "to seize upon those experiences and struggles in which there are still the glimmerings of solidarity and the promise of dialogical communities" (Bernstein 1985:228). Those who are concerned with the plight of dependent people in the modern social welfare state—the poor, minorities, women, the handicapped, the ill—must believe that communities and trust based on goodwill can be created. This is not to argue that society as a whole will or should be organized along communitarian lines—a matter which will be discussed shortly—but certainly in a great many areas human relations ought to be reconstituted.

In the examples that I have chosen, where there is the instrumental creation of community, there are special characteristics that limit their generalizability. They involve heavily professionalized services with professional norms and commitments for care and respect, which should not be underestimated. In addition, the clients do not suffer stigma, at least in a serious way. Even given these characteristics, I emphasize the role of reciprocal mutual concrete incentives in establishing the possibility of the dialogic relationship. There have to be both understanding and cooperation if the professionals are to be able to perform their tasks. In the next chapter, I treat more fully the material and social conditions for dialogism, but state now that I think it highly problematic that naturally dominating professionals (the physician, the teacher, the case manager) would treat the clients as equal moral agents without these reciprocal concrete incentives. Concrete incentives become the basis for reciprocity. As previously discussed, the idea of concrete incentives fits comfortably with the ideas of those who urge a cooperative style of regulation or cooperative styles of bargaining and negotiation, but, somehow, seems inconsistent with the communitarian feminists or the dialogians. Ferguson and the critical philosphers speak of fundamental moral qualities—respect, dignity, caring, nurturing, altruism—rather than of the withholding of sanctions, enrollment in programs, and reporting on the quality of a home help aide. Can there be an ideal speech situation with professionals, officials, and concrete incentives? If reciprocal concrete incentives are necessary, are we really talking about instrumental cooperation rather than dialogism?

I do not view the ideal speech situation as a condition that is finally reached, the arrival of a stabilized relationship in human affairs (Habermas 1970; Rorty 1989). Rather, it is, and always will be, a dynamic, evolving, and digressing condition: a matter of degree, of graduation, of more or less, of points on a continuum (Cornell 1987a). The examples in this book that illustrate situations where there is at least some degree of moral trust also contain some element of the ideal speech situation. There is some degree of contextualization, some degree of listening, and some degree of treating the other as an equal moral agent. At one end of the spectrum, these elements might only constitute a trace, a far cry from what Ferguson and Habermas have in mind. But if we look at what I would regard as some of the middle positions—informed consent with the renal dialysis patient, the Madison special education program, and some of the interactions with the frail, elderly poor—then I think that we see stronger elements and we are farther along the continuum. In the life-world *of these interactions*, there is more autonomy, trust, and respect in the social bond. The moral values of the communitarian feminists and the modern/postmodern ethical philosophers are not submerged by the concrete incentives, because the concrete incentives cannot materialize without the humane values; there have to be respect, dignity, caring, and listening in order for there to be understanding and cooperation. And if there are not *both* understanding and cooperation, if there is not morally based trust, then there will not be reciprocity. But these conditions are not stable. There are no sharp breaks between the instrumental, sentimental, and strong communities. Progress is neither hopeless nor inevitable. If we believe in the importance of context, of the situated individual, then we must also believe in fluidity and change. Trust and genuine dialogue are fragile. Beliefs and actions about oneself and others will always be in flux.

These examples are small. They are tiny corners of the modern social welfare state. Moreover, they are not necessarily all-encompassing of the particular participants, although for the chronically ill and the frail elderly poor, they may be. For the parents of the handicapped children, the special education program is an important part of their lives, but certainly the parents have many other spheres of activity. Is it possible, then, to have an ideal speech situation or a strong community in only a portion of one's life? Ferguson thinks that the communitarian feminist community is inconsistent with modern capitalist bureaucracy. There are several reasons why I think it important to recognize partial communities. At a societal level, one of the basic arguments of the Continental theorists is the importance of self-reflexive subsystems. Habermas does not believe that the rationality potential of communicative action can carry the whole load of societal integration and that other subsystems (e.g., economic, bureaucratic) have to be complementary. The coordinated subsystems presuppose each other. While communicative structures assume a crucial role for rational, democratic control, they are not all-inclusive.

At the micro level, there are also strong arguments for the partial community. A major concern that is always raised about community is the loss of autonomy; individualism becomes subordinate to—

indeed, becomes indistinguishable from—group values (Friedman; Young). All of the communitarians discussed in this paper are sensitive to this issue; all take great pains to qualify the relationship of the individual to others, to allow for self-reflexion, and for some measure of cognitive and behavioral distance. This means that one must be free to leave the community; otherwise autonomy is an illusion (Unger). What is contemplated, then, is not one, all-inclusive community for some aspects of one's life. In a complex society, there are multiple occasions for communicative action. These examples are designed to illustrate community in one aspect of the lives of dependent people. But for these people, there are probably other aspects of their lives where they are not dependent.

There is also a strategic reason for looking for partial communities, the "glimmerings of solidarity." If we are engaged in the struggle to reconstitute the relationship of dependent people to the state, then unless we know how to get from here to there, it would seem that steps have to be taken along the way. The daily struggle to search out, create, and nurture humane relations between people means, of course, partial communities can be created in selected aspects of life.

There is also an aesthetic objection to the kind of community for which I am arguing. As Eagleton and Bernstein have pointed out, dialogians have not paid attention to the issue of power. Another way of stating this—a bit more harshly—is that there tends to be an elitist, romantic strain in the vision of community. Perhaps reflecting its origins in utopian, rural communities, the word "community" conjures visions of cultured, civilized, well-educated, well-endowed, strong, healthy—and yes, white—adults and young children joining together in a sylvan, self-sufficient rural setting, growing vegetables and weaving cloth. In discussing community, one does not ordinarily think of sick, frightened people connected to machines for life, or guilt-stricken, confused, lower-class, minority parents trying to understand a formidable, opaque school bureaucracy, or a frail, poor old woman trying to live out her remaining days with dignity. But it is in the grubby halls of bureaucracy that the poor and disadvantaged live. These are some of the people that Baier speaks of. Can we create Bernstein's regulative ideal at the bottom end of the structure of power?

We are concerned with the creation and nurturing of dialogic communities for dependent people in their relations with the state. These communities, if successful, will be both partial and necessarily unstable. While I think that many situations might be reconstituted along communitarian lines, it must be recognized that there are major important programs that involve dependent people but will probably not be amenable to this approach. We will discuss these additional limits on generalizability after we consider the material and social conditions necessary for the communities represented in even my small-scale examples.

Chapter 7
The Material and Social Conditions of Community

The foundational condition of dialogism lies in the predisposition of the parties—they must want to and be able to enter into a conversation. In some situations, cooperation may be based on mutual deterrence, or naked instrumentalism, but such cases would be rare, and unimportant for our concerns. Even Axelrod thinks that "nice guys" are better off in tit for tat. Hawkins's example works when there is a predisposition to trust, and trusting states of mind are, of course, absolutely essential for the three participatory examples; at this point in the argument, we can take this condition as given. What will allow this trust to take root and to flourish?

Professional Norms

Our concern is with the relationship of dependent people to bureaucracies. First, we will consider the conditions of dialogism from the perspective of the agency worker; then, we will turn to the client.
There are two major structural characteristics of the line staff; both are interrelated. One is that the staff is part of a bureaucratic organization, more particularly for our purposes, a human service organization. Recall, then, Hasenfeld's discussion about the characteristics of organizations, and particularly how the agency workers develop practice ideologies to enhance their survival needs as

organizational participants. Their goals may or may not coincide with the goals of the clients. The structure of the service technology selects, sorts, routes, and treats clients in terms of the needs of the agency and staff. The second characteristic is that the agency workers are either professionals or purport to adopt professional norms and ideologies. This, of course, is not true for many large-scale income-maintenance programs, but we will assume it to be true for many of the human service organizations with which we are now concerned. This means that dialogism has to become a part of professional norms; we cannot ask professionals to violate their own principles.

In the three participatory examples, dialogism was consistent with professional norms—but these were unusual examples. Informed consent as dialogism is rare in standard medicine. While the law mandates informed consent, it does not qualify as dialogism; because the medical profession does not believe in dialogism as included in their professional norms, doctors only obey the law. In special education, the failure of dialogism is both professional and bureaucratic. Most school personnel do not think that parents have anything significant to tell them. This is the standard model of professional-client interactions—the professional or expert has the knowledge, the training, and the experience. In addition, special-education personnel usually think that parents are part of the problem. Even in the community care for the frail, elderly poor, prior to the recent demonstration projects, the case manager–client relationship was hierarchical. The workers dispensed services to those who applied. As Hasenfeld shows, the legal-bureaucratic practice is widespread in human service organizations (Hasenfeld 1983).

In reaction to the legal-bureaucratic regime, William Simon has urged the idea of "downward professionalism." Simon is responding to the changes in the welfare system over the past twenty-five years that can be characterized as formalization, bureaucratization, and proletarianization (Simon 1983, 1985, 1986). While many factors, of course, have produced this state of affairs, Simon emphasizes the ideological and administrative combination of Weberian efficiency and the legal rights approach which insisted that relationships between clients and welfare agencies be governed by entitlements and strict rules; discretion be reduced as much as possible; and client interests be protected by procedural due process. The legal rights approach reacted to what it considered to be the arbitrary, moralistic, intrusive, and often punitive imposition of values by traditional social work practice. Discretion—informality, decentralization, and professionalism—was the enemy.

While conceding that there were many abuses of what purported to be social work practice in a highly discretionary system, Simon argues that social work practice theory, as developed by the most prominent theoreticians and practitioners in and around the New Deal period, has been seriously misrepresented: if properly understood, the theory could be seen to be highly responsive to the rights and dignity of welfare clients and, moreover, it serves as an apt model for contemporary reform. There are strong elements of dialogism in this early social work practice theory, including a particularly progressive view of the function of rights. As part of progressivism, the earlier social workers rejected the rigid individualism of classical liberalism and, instead, embraced the idea of "interdependence." Interdependence had two components: first, that in the modern, complex, industrial society, material well-being depends on extensive and complex cooperation; and second, that individuality is a social and cultural phenomenon, and that in order for a person to be independent, he or she must be recognized and respected as such by others. Mutual dependence was not a regrettable burden of modern life; rather, it was "a morally valuable and fulfilling aspect of the human condition. . . . Both cooperation and recognition require a substantial degree of trust and solidarity" (Simon 1986:1437).

The social workers' idea of rights fits into this concept of interdependence, autonomy, and cooperation. Rights were not categorical trumps that ended conversation, but were dialectic; validity depended upon consequences for others; competing norms and values were reconciled and compromised. Rights were used to facilitate conversation. In Simon's phrase, rights had a *regenerative character*. By this he means that the autonomy of the client is a goal rather than the premise of classical liberalism. The social workers did not take the client's capacities as given, but as something to be enhanced by the legal system. For example, fair hearings (which, as Simon points out, were introduced in welfare in the New Deal period), should be not be used to reject claims but as an opportunity to assess the claimant's judgment, trustworthiness, and the merits of her opinion. The enforcement of rights was to help people to define and effectuate their goals, to foster a general sense of self-respect and autonomy. Clients should be made to feel comfortable and treated with respect. They were presumed to be eligible. In order to discourage dependency, clients themselves should aid in the eligibility process. Clients were to be given information not only about the particular agency, but also about the availability of alternatives, and the worker was to help the client in seeking other alternatives, if indicated. Finally, the client was encouraged to pursue a more reflective and articulate understanding of her interests through extended conversation with the worker. The conversation would continue until the worker and the client felt confident that a sound understanding was reached or until the client decided to terminate the relationship (Minow).

The workers were not expected to be neutral in this conversation. This did not mean lack of respect for client autonomy; rather, it was a recognition of the possibility that the social context was conditioning the client's perception of her own interests. Neutrality, it was felt, would inhibit the conversation, the ability to challenge the client to develop individual ideas about self-interests; but it was also important for the worker to appear as a distinct individual who has ideas and is capable of empathy and feelings of solidarity. Disdaining neutrality did not mean, in the workers' view, embracing paternalism. The client had the choice to engage in the conversation and to make whatever decisions emerged.

The social workers saw no incompatibility between the therapeutic aspects of the relationship and the emphasis on claimant rights. Teaching the claimant to regard herself as a rightholder was a means of enhancing her self-confidence and dignity. It was also a way of enabling the client to respond to and learn from the worker without being oppressed by her. Rights rhetoric was a defense against worker oppression. (Simon 1985:20)

The social worker practice theorists expected a lot from the workers. Workers were to become personally involved without losing detachment. They were to provide help without encouraging dependency. They were to make judgments but not impose judgments. As with the clients, these norms were goals, something to be striven for in the process. In trying to achieve these goals, there were two dangers or temptations: to apply coercive manipulation or to retreat into bureaucratic formalism. The dangers would be countered by continued professionalism. Worker instruction would continue by means of their distinctive notion of supervision, which paralleled the worker-client relation. The supervisor, in the same office, would have extensive knowledge of the cases and would engage in a continuous dialogue with the worker concerning interpretations and decisions. As with the client, this would be a noncoercive, therapeutic relationship designed to heighten awareness. The provision of material assistance would be integrated into the counseling services. Material assistance would be varied and be responsive to the client's individual circumstances. The worker judgments, in sum, would be informal but complex; they would be set in an administration that was decentralized and professional.

Simon points out that a great deal of what the early social workers were talking about resonates with contemporary ideas, particularly the communitarian feminist belief that personhood is defined through the processes of human interaction. Ferguson says that the feminist vision of human interaction can only be accomplished in a legal system that is decentralized and contextualized and deals with concrete situations.

There are strong elements of dialogism in Simon's concept of professionalism. In addition to the emphasis on *engaged* conversation, where the client and the worker challenge the contextual definition of interests, the ideas of dialogism come out most clearly in Simon's critique of the legal rights approach to welfare administration. While his critique is complex, Simon particularly criticizes the use of rights as categorical trumps, the end of conversation. "Appeals to right occur only when activities and goals conflict; their function is to determine whose side the state will take" (Simon 1985:29). Simon's interpretation of the social workers' vision is that through dialogue, interests can become reconciled and there can be a mutuality of goals.

We can see instances of what Simon refers to in two of the participatory examples. In the Madison School special education program, the leadership worked out an alternative method of special education wherein the parents would be involved and, over the years, they were able to recruit teachers and other special education specialists who agreed with their philosophy. While the previous teachers and special education personnel were also professionals, a new kind of professional with different ideologies had to be recruited. The same is happening in the social agencies that are providing community care for the frail, elderly poor. The leadership realizes that different practices are called for, and they recruit case managers who believe, as professionals, in the new methods. Simon's idea is to extend this kind of professionalism, exemplified by the early social work practice theorists, down to the line staff (Garth); I agree. I think that it is uncontroversial that leadership and downward professionalism are essential (Sabatier and Mazmanian). The professional staff, down to the street-level worker, has to believe that dialogism is an integral part of the professional task; otherwise, the dialogue will be a sham. The law, even the bureaucratic leadership, can mandate a conversation; but they cannot make it happen unless the line participants want it to happen.

Simon, of course, is appealing to the highest ideals of professionalism:

[Its] distinctive ethical orientation toward work. . . . views work as expressing and implementing values that rise above the competing ends of antagonistic individuals and groups. It repudiates the ideal of work as instrumental to the satisfaction of private ends or as a means of imposing one's will on the world and asserts an ideal of work as an intrinsically satisfying form of participation in the life of the community. It is this transcendent, universalistic orientation to work that requires and makes possible autonomy and responsibility in the organization of professional work. (Simon 1983:1256)

It is easy and, I think, cynical, to reject this vision as wildly inconsistent with the practicing professions as we know them today. We have seen a different style of professionalism in the three participatory examples, and, as Simon illustrates, there is a long tradition of high standards in professionalism.

Power, Structure, and Client Self-Determination

There are two major assumptions of the early social work practice theory which must be examined. One is client self-determination;

Decentralization and the Fostering of Discretion

The kind of relation called for between the worker and the dependent client requires fundamental changes in the ideology, structure, and organization of public programs. Simon's downward professionalism, Hasenfeld's empowerment, reciprocal concrete incentives, and dialogism all require discretion at the field level. In order for the participants to engage in meaningful conversation, to explore alternatives, or to exit, there must be arenas that allow freedom of movement. There must be informalism instead of rigid rules; decentralization instead of hierarchical control and professional autonomy. This idea connects with our earlier discussions about the calls for cooperative styles of regulation, alternative dispute resolution, especially the problem-solving style of negotiation, and the Continental jurisprudential theorists who called for reflexive law. Law must become constitution instead of medium to allow for dialogue.

This reconception of the structure of law and administration calls for a rethinking of law, bureaucracy, and the role of social movement organizations. All present concepts create impediments to the dialogic community. The ideology of law and public policy—the Weberian legal-administrative conception—is the rational, bureaucratic, top-down theory of policy formulation and implementation. Laws are formulated by the policymakers and then are implemented. This is the commonsense approach. One starts with an analysis of the policymakers' intent and then examines the steps that are taken through the various implementing agencies to compare outcomes with intent (Elmore). The conceptual framework assumes that rationality, neutrality, and predictability are the norm; it incorporates the rule of law ideology. This ideology abhors discretion; if discretion is necessary, it is a necessary evil, to be watched closely and confined. This ideology cuts sharply against the cooperative style of regulation and favors the strict application of uniform rules.

The top-down framework works only marginally at best, and in human services agencies it is more the exception than the rule. Generally, the bureaucracy is able to deflect the implementation thrust and convert law and regulation to its own ends. As Hasenfeld points out, organizations, especially human service organizations, are not, in fact, pyramidlike structures wherein commands emanate from the top and are implemented throughout the lower levels. Rather, following the political economy model, organizations are arenas of shifting coalitions of power, both internal and external to the organization. The goal of the various groups is survival, which may or may not coincide with the particular commands of the law, let alone the interests of the clients. It is the combination of these two elements—the liberal legal, Weberian ideology of law and administration, and bureaucratic behavior—that contribute to the kinds of pathologies that the Continental theories identified.

The Continental theorists suggest the legal-administrative structural conditions of the dialogic community. Structures must allow sufficient space for associated individuals to engage in the dialogue. This involves taking a positive view of discretion. Recent implementation theory takes this approach. Richard Elmore has argued for "backward mapping" instead of traditional "forward mapping." Forward mapping assumes the ability of the leadership to control the implementation process. Elmore argues that if one views the efforts of those at the top as contingent, as only one factor among many in the process of social change, then backward mapping will more accurately describe the process. Backward mapping looks at the environment within which the field-level agencies are operating. Following the political economy model of organizations, it assumes a loosely coupled, poorly integrated social system of relatively autonomous agencies with different sources of information, perceptions, and goals. It assumes a decentralized system with large amounts of discretion at the field level (Elmore).

According to Elmore, discretion is the more accurate picture. This being the case, what is called for is the recognition of the inevitability of discretion; discretion then should be viewed positively, and be structured more in line with realistic policy goals (Handler and Zatz). In our terms, it means structuring discretion so that it fosters community rather than the legal-bureaucratic regime.

Creating arenas of discretion is, of course, only the first step. The special education statute accomplished this, but instead of effecting participation by the parties, bureaucratic rationalization took over. Within the arenas of discretion, different approaches must be used with the bureaucracy and the participants. It will be recalled (Chapter 3) that one of the most important characteristics of the loosely coupled, political economy model was the environment; as open systems, competing groups within the bureaucracy seek to control environmental resources as a way of enhancing their own position. Internally, power within the organization depends on the importance of the units to the operative goals of the organization and the resources that that group can command. Hasenfeld emphasizes the bargains that the organization has to make with other key actors in the environment who control necessary resources.

Organizations do change; in fact, many are in constant flux. The goal is to try to change the organization in the desired direction and then maintain that direction. We start with leadership and then with Simon's downward professionalism—in other words, the conscious recruitment of personnel committed to the program, as was done in the Madison school district. But those actions will not be sustaining unless they are supported by changes in internal incentives. For example, one of the key problems in public human services agencies involves the reimbursement formulae. Although the reimbursement formulae in special education are complex and varied, in general they militate against the Madison decision-making processes; that is, school districts are reimbursed on the basis of the number of students in particular slots. This means that speedy, efficient placement decisions and continuation in the slot are rewarded and careful, patient conversations and reevaluations are penalized. Health care professionals complain of similar problems. Physicians are compensated by units; they are not paid to have the careful conversations that genuine informed consent entails. On the other hand, the reimbursement formula aided conversation with the frail, elderly poor; the agencies could not stay within their financial constraints unless they enlisted the active cooperation of the clients and their informal care-givers.

Intimately connected with the reimbursement formula is the issue of accountability. Accountability is substantively important. These programs deal with dependent, vulnerable people who are often victimized, and there is an important public interest in their protection. The programs spend a lot of money, and there is an important interest in reducing waste and abuse. However, as

Hasenfeld points out, it is often difficult and expensive for top management to find out precisely what is going on between the worker and the client. Consequently, there is great pressure to standardize the operations using objectively verifiable units of inputs and process—the number and kind of patients seen, the specific procedures, the number of students processed, the number and hours of home help aides, and so forth. Mandated quantitative reports provide managers with some information, but the effects of this kind of monitoring are profound in shaping lower-level activities. Great distortions are often produced in order to meet statistically imposed quotas. The staff shapes its activities for statistical compliance, which may or may not coincide with other, more important public goals. These internal control mechanisms are important for they are major sources of dysfunction and bureaucratic rationalization; they must be changed to encourage different styles of professional behavior, but they are resistant to change because of the importance of Weberian, legalistic, top-down, command-and-control ideology. Just how one should reward patient, careful, dialogue is not self-evident, but, at least, dialogue must not be penalized, as it is under present regimes.

Hasenfeld suggests that client feedback can be an important empowerment-accountability tool. We saw that this was the case with the frail, elderly poor, where client and care-giver information served two purposes: it empowered clients because they now had a resource that the agency needed, but it also carried important regulatory implications. With dependent clients, the supervising agency has to generate all of the information; this is an important impetus for strict monitoring. One of the benefits of creating dialogic communities in the administration of programs is that the clients themselves become an important source of information, thus altering this important regulatory task. To the extent that there is good client feedback, the supervising agency has better, more reliable information than top-down, mandated objective reports. I will return to this point again after discussing ways of enhancing client participation.

The environment must be altered to support and encourage the new professionals. Of course, there must be adequate resources to do so. If case loads are extremely heavy and contract support services are not available, then there is little that the workers can do (Garth 1986–87). There will be enormous pressure to get through the day, to at least say something to those patiently waiting for appointments, but there will be few choices to make participation meaningful. Conversely, to the extent that the new professionals can command both internal and external resources, they will be successful in the organization. These points are obvious. The organizations and their environments have to be changed if Simon's new professionals are to survive.

At this point in the analysis, I have discussed changes in law and administration along reflexive lines which will create arenas where dialogism can take place. In addition, the bureaucracy has been changed in that it is now staffed with the new professionals who have reconceived their professional tasks along dialogic or client-empowerment lines. The posture of the law and the bureaucracy cannot be overemphasized. In the situations that we refer to—dependent people dealing with public agencies—the field-level staff must be committed to genuine conversation, *and* they must be supported by the legal and bureaucratic systems; otherwise I doubt very much whether dialogism will ever occur.

The legal rights experience of the 1960s and 1970s is still sobering. Legal rights of participation were granted to clients and they were to enforce those rights through the adversary system. But, in general, clients lacked the resources, and the bureaucracy proved to be too powerful. Legal rights attempts to strengthen clients, but one of the great mistakes of the legal rights revolution as well as of contemporary reforms, such as alternative dispute resolution, is the failure to take account of the issue of power. The forces that largely scuttled the legal rights revolution in the situations that I have discussed will surely reproduce themselves in alternative dispute resolution as well as in other changes made to encourage dialogism that do not take account of structure and power. This is why I lay such great store in not only the new professionalism but also the development of mutual reciprocal concrete incentives to reinforce the moral predispositions of the professionals. The combination changes the posture of the bureaucracy in a fundamental way: instead of being hostile adversaries to client demands for participation, bureaucrats are offering to share power. Moreover, they are offering to share power not only for the moral values of dialogism, but also because they *need* the understanding and active participation of the clients.

Empowering Clients

Can the clients participate within this framework of opportunity? It depends. One would think that the renal dialysis patients would be more able to assimilate the information and take advantage of the invitation, indeed the demand, to take part than the special education parents, and that the parents would be more able than the frail, elderly poor. Generally speaking, the more dependent the client is to begin with (other factors being equal), the more the client's ability to participate is in doubt. But surely feelings of powerlessness, of being overwhelmed, cannot be generalized across categories of dependency; there must be enormous individual variation that calls for sensitive, contextualized judgment. The larger point, however, is that dominating relationships are not solely the doing of the professional. Professionals who try to increase client involvement report great difficulty in getting the client involved and, often, in exasperation, cannot resist telling the client what they think is the best course of action (Wexler).

Clients, then, especially dependent clients, must be given resources; both Simon and Hasenfeld call on the workers to help clients obtain resources. Social movement groups are important resources. There is a long history of social movement groups; many were and are quite successful. While the intense activism of the 1960s and early 1970s has subsided, there are still countless groups still functioning, some nationally and regionally, and many locally in the communities. They vary in terms of size, organizational strength, and goals. Some are very important politically; others virtually small social clubs (Boyte 1980; Handler 1986).

However, within the population that we are talking about, social movement groups are more problematic. It has always proved to be more difficult to organize and maintain groups as one moves down the socioeconomic scale. There are a variety of reasons for this difficulty, principally having to do with incentives. Groups with more affluent members, naturally, can offer more selective incentives (e.g., insurance and other kinds of individually consumed goods) and seem to generate greater responses to purposive appeals—for example, wilderness preservation. On the other hand, the research producing these data is based on lower-class groups facing traditional bureaucracies where payoffs are extremely hard to extract. The ability to mobilize could change if the payoffs increased. We notice this, for example, with black electoral behavior. When something was at stake for blacks (municipal elections and the Jesse Jackson campaign), electoral activity not only increased, but, controlling for socioeconomic class, actually now surpasses whites. But even with the presence of black candidates, the increase in black voting did not come automatically; there had to be organization, registration drives, and a great deal of other kinds of social movement activity.

In our situation, there is also an increase in payoff. As the clients participate, however haltingly, there are the invitations, the patient wooing, the respect. Again recall the quote from the Madison parent who remarked that the teachers never criticized her, they always encouraged her. Nevertheless, it would still seem that dependent people would need more resources. Madison recognized this. They offered parent advocates, not for adversarial advocacy but for *communicative* advocacy, to negotiate etiquette barriers. Parents also had the opportunity to retain their own experts. Still, this was not enough. For a time, the state department of education conducted training sessions for parents. Small stipends, day care, and meals were provided. Not only were the law and the programs explained, but the parents were also given assertiveness training. At this time, there were also active parent groups. This was the period of social activism on behalf of handicapped children, and while these groups were usually led and staffed by middle-class parents, all were encouraged to participate at the local level; their common interests in public special education crossed class lines.

It is not accidental that the Madison school staff reports that in those days parent participation was at a higher level than today. Subsequently, for a variety of reasons, the groups withered. Part of the reason may have been a form of systemwide co-optation; reforms were successful, the district and the teachers were more than responsive, indeed, ahead of the demands, and there were important, tangible, substantive successes. In any event, the staff today reports much more passiveness on the part of parents and more difficulty in getting parents to question, participate, and work with the school instead of accepting teacher recommendations. They blame this, in part, on the decline of the social movement groups.

Social movement groups, in these situations, perform a variety of functions. At the most basic level, they show people that they are not alone and that they are not necessarily victims, but others share their burdens. New renal dialysis patients are introduced to other patients. There also have been successful groups established for informal care-givers of the frail elderly and for adult children of nursing-home residents. The importance of this sharing, this banding together if only for comfort, cannot be overestimated. The members share information, they hear stories from more experienced members, and they offer each other support. In the process, they collectivize grievances and are able to raise systemic problems. Both of these functions, the uncovering of individual and systemic problems, are important sources of information for the agency. It was shown in Chapter 6 that, in demonstration projects for the frail, elderly poor, the importance of social movement groups was recognized. The agencies try to encourage the clients and their families to get together and form their own groups. In large part, the purpose of the groups is to share burdens—for example, groups of informal care-givers who meet to talk about their individual psychological needs—but problems with the programs are raised. Nevertheless, it must be recognized that it is difficult to form such groups, especially when the elderly poor person is alone.

If dependent clients, then, are to participate effectively, social movement groups are important. The clients need the strength of the group for their individual participation, and the agency also needs the groups not only to strengthen the client, but also to provide important information. In other words, participating clients *and* social movement groups are incorporated into the implementation framework. This is a change from standard implementation theory, which is usually limited to the chain of command and sometimes includes the client. The professional task has been reconceptualized to include the client as part of the solution, but for this to work, the social movement group also has to be part of the solution.

Despite the receptivity to group activity, most groups will probably need outside support. This raises the problem of co-optation.

As a result of the War on Poverty, there rose the phenomenon of the mandated citizen group. In practically all major federal legislation that shares resources with state and local governments, some form of citizen groups had to be created. The selection, composition, and function of these groups vary; some only advise, others actually deliver services. They act as intermediaries between the citizen and officials. On the whole, however, they do not act as independent sources of information; rather, they serve to legitimize the agencies (Handler 1986).

This, of course, can happen to the groups envisaged here. They can be manipulated and co-opted by the agencies, but this would be self-defeating. The central idea of these groups is to strengthen the client and to strengthen the independence of the group so that the staff and the agency can better perform their tasks. The group is not viewed by the agency as an enemy or as a source of legitimacy, but as a source of information. To be a reliable source of information, it must remain independent. The social agencies that deal with the frail, elderly poor realize this. Although it has been difficult to get these groups going and to nurture them, their importance and independence has been recognized. In Madison, the importance of social movement groups was never fully appreciated; and partly for this reason, parent participation has weakened.

Annette Baier emphasizes the fragility of trust. What we are trying to accomplish is equal moral agency in a greatly unequal world. This is no small task. Even for the small encounters that I am talking about—small in the societal sense but large in the lives of these particular clients—the dialogic community requires an extensive reconceptualization and restructuring of the way we conduct our public business. The ideas tie together. To allow for conversation between the professional and the client, the law and the bureaucracy must create the arenas for the conversation. This requires a different way of thinking about the structure and design of our major public social welfare programs. But opportunity is not enough. Support is needed for the agency, for its staff, and for the participating clients; they all need a supporting environment. Most of our ideologies, traditions, and practices run in opposite directions; yet, the task is not hopeless. There are many examples where varying degrees of dialogism take place.

References

Abel, Emily (1987), *Love Is Not Enough: Family Care of the Frail Elderly* (Washington, D.C.: American Public Health Policy Series).
Abel, Richard (1985), "Risk as an Arena of Struggle," *Michigan Law Review*, Vol. 83: 772–812.
———, ed. (1982), *The Politics of Informal Justice*, Vols. 1, 2 (New York: Academic Press).
Ackerman, Bruce, and Richard Stewart (1985), "Reforming Environmental Law," *Stanford Law Review*, Vol. 37: 1333–1365.
Adler, Michael, and Stewart Asquith, eds. (1981), *Discretion and Welfare* (London: Heinemann Educational Books).
Altman, Andrew (1986), "Legal Realism, Critical Legal Studies, and Dworkin," *Philosophy and Public Affairs*, Vol. 15: 205–235.
Axelrod, Robert (1984), *The Evolution of Cooperation* (New York: Basic Books).
Bachrach, Peter, and Morton Baratz (1962), "The Two Faces of Power," *American Political Science Review* 56: 947–952.
——— (1970), *Power and Poverty: Theory and Practice* (New York: Oxford University Press).
Baier, Annette (1986), "Trust and Antitrust," *Ethics*, Vol. 96: 231–260.
Baker, C. Edwin (1985), "Sandel on Rawls," *University of Pennsylvania Law Review*, Vol. 133: 895–928.
Barber, Bernard (1983), *The Logic and Limits of Trust* (New Brunswick, N.J.: Rutgers University Press).
Bardach, Eugene, and Robert Kagan (1982), *Going by the Book: The Problem of Regulatory Unreasonableness* (Philadelphia: Temple University Press).
Beauchamp, Tom L., and James F. Childress (1983), *Principles of Biomedical Ethics*, 2nd ed. (New York: Oxford University Press).
Bell, Derrick (1987), *And We Are Not Saved: The Elusive Quest for Racial Justice* (New York: Basic Books).

Bernstein, Richard (1976), *The Restructuring of Social and Political Theory* (New York: Harcourt Brace Jovanovich).

——— (1985), *Beyond Objectivism and Relativism: Science, Hermeneutics, and Praxis* (Philadelphia: University of Pennsylvania Press).

——— (1986), *Philosophical Profiles: Essays in a Pragmatic Mode* (Cambridge: Polity Press).

———, ed. (1985), *Habermas and Modernity* (Cambridge: MIT Press).

Boyd, Robert, and Jeffery Loberbaum (1987), "No Pure Strategy Is Evolutionarily Stable in the Repeated Prisoner's Dilemma Game," *Nature*, Vol. 327: 58–59.

Boyte, Harry (1980), *The Backyard Revolution: Understanding the New Citizen's Movement* (Philadelphia: Temple University Press).

Brigham, John (1987), "Rights, Rage, and Remedy: The Construction of Legal Discourse," *Studies in American Political Development*, Vol. 2: 303–316.

Brodkin, Evelyn (1987), "Policy Politics: If We Can't Govern, Can We Manage?" *Political Science Quarterly*, Vol. 102: 571–587.

Bumiller, Kristin (1988), *The Civil Rights Society: The Social Construction of Victims* (Baltimore: Johns Hopkins University Press).

Bush, Robert (1989), "Defining Quality in Dispute Resolution Taxonomies and Anti-Taxonomies of Quality Arguments," *Denver University Law Review*, Vol. 66: 335–380.

Butler, Patricia (1980), "A Long-Term Care Strategy for Legal Services," *Clearinghouse Review, Special Issue*, Vol. 14: 613–701.

Christman, John (1988), "Constructing the Inner Citadel: Recent Work on the Concept of Autonomy," *Ethics*, Vol. 99: 109–124.

Clune, William (1987), "Legal Disintegration and a Theory of the State," Institute for Legal Studies, Working Paper, Series 2:5. Madison: University of Wisconsin–Madison Law School, Feb. 1987.

Clune, William, and Mark Van Pelt (1985), "A Political Method of Evaluating 94–142 and the Several Gaps of Gap Analysis," *Law and Contemporary Problems*, Vol. 48: 7–62.

Coates, Dan, and Steven Penrod (1980–81), "Social Psychology and the Emergence of Disputes," *Law and Society Review*, Vol. 15: 655–680.

Connolly, William (1983), *The Terms of Political Discourse*, 2nd ed. (Princeton: Princeton University Press).

Cornell, Drucilla (1985), "Toward a Modern/Postmodern Reconstruction of Ethics," *University of Pennsylvania Law Review*, Vol. 133: 291–380.

——— (1987a), "The Poststructuralist Challenge to the Ideal of Community," *Cardozo Law Review*, Vol. 8: 989–1022.

——— (1987b), "In Union: A Critical Review of *Toward a Perfected State*," *University of Pennsylvania Law Review*, Vol. 135: 1089–1121.

Crenshaw, Kimberlé (1988), "Race, Reform, and Retrenchment: Transformation and Legitimation in Antidiscrimination Law," *Harvard Law Review*, Vol. 101: 1331–1387.

Dahl, Robert (1986), "Power as the Control of Behavior," in Steven Lukes, ed., *Power* (New York: New York University Press): 37–58.

Dalton, Harlon (1987), "The Clouded Prism," *Harvard Civil Rights–Civil Liberties Law Review*, Vol. 22: 435–447.

Delgado, Richard (1987), "The Ethereal Scholar: Does Critical Legal Studies Have What Minorities Want?" *Harvard Civil Rights–Civil Liberties Law Review*, Vol. 22: 301–322.

Delgado, Richard, et al. (1985), "Fairness and Formality: Minimizing the Risk of Prejudice in Alternative Dispute Resolution," *Wisconsin Law Review*, 1359–1404.

Dobrof, Rose [1985], "Community Involvement: An Approach to Enforcement of Quality of Life in Nursing Homes" (paper prepared for the Institute of Medicine Committee on Nursing Home Regulation, Fredericksburg, Va., Dec. 10–12, mimeo).

Doty, Pamela, and Ellen Sullivan (1983), "Community Involvement in Combating Abuse, Neglect, and Mistreatment in Nursing Homes," *Milbank Memorial Fund Quarterly/Health and Society*, Vol. 16: 222–251.

Eagleton, Terry (1983), *Literary Theory: An Introduction* (Minneapolis: University of Minnesota Press).

Edelman, Murray (1971), *Politics as Symbolic Action: Mass Arousal and Quiescence* (Chicago: Markham Publishing Co.).

Elmore, Richard (1978), "Organizational Modes of Social Program Implementation," *Public Policy*, Vol. 26: 185–228.

——— (1980), "Backward Mapping: Implementation Research and Policy Decisions," *Political Science Quarterly*, Vol. 94: 601–616.

Felstiner, William, Richard Abel, and Austin Sarat (1980), "The Emergence and Transformation of Disputes: Naming, Blaming, Claiming...," *Law and Society Review*, Vol. 15, 3–4: 631–654.

Ferguson, Kathy (1984), *The Feminist Case Against Bureaucracy* (Philadelphia: Temple University Press).

Foucault, Michel (1980), *Power/Knowledge: Selected Interviews and Other Writings*, Colin Gordon, ed. (New York: Pantheon).

——— (1986), "Disciplinary Power and Subjection," in Steven Lukes, ed., *Power* (New York: New York University Press): 229–242.

Freeman, Alan (1988), "Responses to the Minority Critiques of the Critical Legal Studies Movement," *Harvard Civil Rights–Civil Liberties Law Review*, Vol. 23: 295–392.

Freire, Paulo (1985), *Pedagogy of the Oppressed* (New York: Continuum).

Friedman, Marilyn (1989), "Feminism and Modern Friendship: Dislocating the Community," *Ethics*, Vol. 99: 275–290.

Frug, Gerald (1984), "The Ideology of Bureaucracy in American Law," *Harvard Law Review*, Vol. 97: 1276–1388.

Frug, Mary Jo (1987), The Role of Difference Models in the Study of Women in Law (unpublished manuscript).

Gabel, Peter (1989), "The Transformative Possibilities of Legal Culture," *Tikkun*, Vol. 4: 17.

Gabel, Peter, and Duncan Kennedy (1984), "Roll Over Beethoven," *Stanford Law Review*, Vol. 36: 1–55.

Galanter, Marc (1983), "Reading the Landscape of Disputes: What We Know and Don't Know (and Think We Know) About Our Allegedly Contentious and Litigious Society," *UCLA Law Review*, Vol. 31: 4–71.

Gallagher, William (1988), "The Transformation of Justice: Hofrichter's *Neighborhood Justice* and Harrington's *Shadow Justice*," *Law and Social Inquiry*, Vol. 13: 133–154.

Gamson, William (1968), *Power and Discontent* (Homewood, Ill.: Dorsey Press).

Garth, Bryant (1986–87), "Independent Professional Power and the Search for a Legal Ideology with a Progressive Bite," *Indiana Law Review*, Vol. 62: 183–214.

Gaventa, John (1980), *Power and Powerlessness: Quiescence and Rebellion in an Appalachian Valley* (Urbana: University of Illinois Press).

Giddens, Anthony (1985), "Reason Without Revolution? Habermas's *Theorie des kommunikativen Handelns*," in Richard Bernstein, ed., *Habermas and Modernity* (Cambridge: MIT Press): 95–121.

Goldstein, Robert (1988), *Abortion and Mother-Love* (Berkeley: University of California Press).

Gordon, Robert (1984), "Critical Legal Histories," *Stanford Law Review*, Vol. 36: 57–125.

Gramsci, Antonio (1971), *Selection from the Prison Notebooks*, Q. Hoare and G. Smith, trans. (New York: International Publishers).

Habermas, Jürgen (1970), "Towards a Theory of Communicative Competence," *Inquiry*, Vol. 13: 361.

——— (1986a), "Hannah Arendt's Communications Concept of Power," in Steven Lukes, ed., *Power* (New York: New York University Press): 75–93.

——— (1986b), "Law as Medium and Law as Institution," in Gunther Teubner, ed., *Dilemmas of Law in the Welfare State* (Berlin: Walter de Gruyter): 203–220.

——— (1987), *The Theory of Communicative Action*, Vol. 2, *Lifeworld and Systems: A Critique of Functionalist Reason*, John McCarthy, trans. (Boston: Beacon Press).

Hahn, Robert, and Gordon Hester (1989), "Where Did All the Markets Go? An Analysis of EPA's Emissions Trading Program," *Yale Journal on Regulation*, Vol. 6: 109–153.

Handler, Joel (1969), "Justice for the Welfare Recipient: Fair Hearings in AFDC, The Wisconsin Experience," *Social Services Review*, Vol. 43: 12–34.

——— (1986), *The Conditions of Discretion: Autonomy, Community, Bureaucracy* (New York: Russell Sage Foundation).

——— (1987–88), "The Transformation of Aid to Families with Dependent Children: The Family Support Act in Historical Context," *New York University Journal of Law and Social Change*, Vol. 16: 457–533.

——— (1988), "Dependent People, the State, and the Modern/Postmodern Search for the Dialogic Community," *UCLA Law Review*, Vol. 35: 999–1113.

Handler, Joel, and Julie Zatz, eds. (1982), *Neither Angels Nor Thieves* (Washington, D.C.: National Academy of Sciences Press).

Harrington, Christine (1982), "Delegation Reform Movements: A Historical Analysis," in Richard Abel, ed., *The Politics of Informal Justice, Vols. 1, 2* (New York: Academic Press).

——— (1988), "Regulatory Reform: Creating Gaps and Making Markets," *Law and Policy*, Vol. 10: 293–315.

Harrington, Christine, and Sally Merry (1988), "Ideological Production: The Making of Community Mediation," *Law and Society Review*, Vol. 22: 709–735.

Hartmann, Heidi (1987), "Changes in Women's Economic and Family Roles," in Lourdes Beneria and Catherine Stimpson, eds., *Women, Households, and the Economy* (New Brunswick, N.J.: Rutgers University Press): 33–58.

Hasenfeld, Yeheskel (1983), *Human Service Organizations* (Englewood Cliffs, N.J.: Prentice-Hall).

——— (1987), "Power in Social Work Practice," *Social Service Review*, Vol. 61: 469–483.

Hawkins, Keith (1984), *Environment and Enforcement: Regulation and the Social Definition of Pollution* (Oxford: The Clarendon Press).

——— (1986), "On Legal Decision-Making," *Washington and Lee Law Review*, Vol. 43: 1161–1242.

Held, Virginia (1987), "Non-Contractual Society: A Feminist View," *Canadian Journal of Philosophy*, Supp. Vol. 13: 111–137.

Heller, Kirby, Wayne Holtzman, and Samuel Messick, eds. (1982), *Placing Children in Special Education: A Strategy for Equity* (Washington, D.C.: National Academy Press).

Himmelfarb, Gertrude (1984), *The Idea of Poverty* (New York: Alfred Knopf).

Hoy, David (1985), "Jacques Derrida," in Quentin Skinner, ed., *The Return of Grand Theory in the Human Sciences* (Cambridge: Cambridge University Press): 41–64.

Huber, Peter (1983), "Exorcists Vs. Gatekeepers in Risk Regulation," *Regulation*, November/December: 23–32.

Institute of Medicine, Committee on Nursing Home Regulation (1986), *Improving the Quality of Care in Nursing Homes* (Washington, D.C.: National Academy of Sciences Press).

Kagan, Robert (1984), Book Review, "Inside Administration Law," *Columbia Law Review*, Vol. 84: 816.

Katz, Jay (1984), *The Silent World of Doctor and Patient* (New York: Free Press).

Kelman, Mark (1987), *A Guide to Critical Legal Studies* (Cambridge: Harvard University Press).

Kramer, Ralph (1987), "Voluntary Agencies and the Personal Social Services," in Walter Powell, ed., *The Nonprofit Sector: A Research Handbook* (New Haven: Yale University Press): 240–257.

Ladd, John (1970), "Morality and the Ideal of Rationality in Formal Organizations," *The Monist*, Vol. 54: 488–516.

Latin, Howard (1985), "Ideal Versus Real Regulation Efficiency: Implementation of Uniform Standards and 'Fine-Tuning' Regulatory Reforms," *Stanford Law Review*, Vol. 37: 1267–1332.

Lempert, Richard (1980–81), "Grievances and Legitimacy: The Beginnings and End of Dispute Settlement," *Law and Society Review*, Vol. 15: 707–716.

Lidz, Charles, and Alan Meisel (1982), "Informed Consent and the Structure of Medical Care," in the President's Commission for the Study of Ethical Problems in Medicine and Biomedical and Behavioral Research, *Making Health Care Decisions* (Washington, D.C.: U.S. Government Printing Office): 349–353.

Lipsky, Michael (1980), *Street-Level Bureaucracy: Dilemmas of the Individual in Public Services* (New York: Russell Sage Foundation).

Littleton, Christine (1989), "Feminist Jurisprudence: The Difference Method Makes," *Stanford Law Review*, Vol. 41: 751–84.

Luhmann, Niklas (1980), *Trust and Power* (New York: John Wiley).

——— (1985), "The Self-Reproduction of Law and Its Limits," in Gunther Teubner, ed., *Dilemmas of Law in the Welfare State* (Berlin: Walter de Gruyter): 111–127.

——— (1988), "Closure and Openness: On Reality in the World of Law," in Gunther Teubner, ed., *Autopoietic Law: A New Approach to Law and Society* (Berlin: Walter de Gruyter): 335–348.

Lukes, Steven (1974), *Power: A Radical View* (London: MacMillan).

———, ed. (1986), *Power* (New York: New York University Press).

Macaulay, Stewart (1963), "Non-Contractual Relations in Business: A Preliminary Study," *American Sociological Review*, Vol. 28: 55–67.

MacIntyre, Alasdair (1984), "Alasdair MacIntyre: The Virtues, the Unity of a Human Life and the Concept of a Tradition," in Michael Sandel, ed., *Liberalism and Its Critics* (Oxford: Basil Blackwell): 125–147.

MacKinnon, Catharine (1987), *Feminism Unmodified* (Cambridge: Harvard University Press).

Macpherson, C. B. (1962), *The Political Theory of Possessive Individualism: Hobbes to Locke* (London: Oxford University Press).

March, James, and Johan Olsen, eds. (1979), *Ambiguity and Choice in Organizations* (Bergen, Norway: Universitesforlager).

Matsuda, Mari (1987), "Looking to the Bottom: Critical Legal Studies and

Reparations," *Harvard Civil Rights–Civil Liberties Law Review*, Vol. 22: 323–399.
Mead, Lawrence (1986), *Beyond Entitlement: The Social Obligations of Citizenship* (New York: Free Press).
Menkel-Meadow, Carrie (1984), "Toward Another View of Legal Negotiation: The Structure of Problem Solving," *UCLA Law Review*, Vol. 31: 754–842.
——— (1985), "For and Against Settlement: Major Public Policy Issues of Dispute Resolution," *UCLA Law Review*, Vol. 33: 485–514.
——— (1986), "Dispute Resolution: The Periphery Becomes the Core," *Judicature*, Vol. 69: 300–304.
Merry, Sally (1986), "Everyday Understandings of the Law in Working Class America," *American Ethnologist*, Vol. 13: 254–270.
Minow, Martha (1987), "Interpreting Rights: An Essay for Robert Cover," *Yale Law Journal*, Vol. 96: 1860–1915.
Molotch, Harvey, and Deirdre Boden (1985), "Talking Social Structures: Discourse, Domination and the Watergate Hearings," *American Sociological Review*, Vol. 50: 273–288.
Montgomery, Rhonda (1983), "Staff-Family Relations and Institutional Care Policies," *Journal of Gerontological Social Work*, Vol. 6: 25–37.
Nelkin, David (1988), "Changing Paradigms in the Sociology of Law," in Gunther Teubner, ed., *Autopoietic Law: A New Approach to Law and Society* (Berlin: Walter de Gruyter): 191–216.
Noble, Charles (1986), *Liberalism at Work: The Rise and Fall of OSHA* (Philadelphia: Temple University Press).
Norris, Christopher (1988), "Law, Deconstruction, and the Resistance to Theory," *Journal of Law and Society*, Vol. 15: 166–187.
Olsen, Frances (1984), "Statutory Rape: A Feminist Critique of Rights Analysis," *Texas Law Review*, Vol. 63: 387–432.
Parsons, Talcott (1986), "Power and the Social System," in Steven Lukes, ed., *Power* (New York: New York University Press): 94–143.
Peller, Gary (1987), "On Deconstruction," *Tikkun*, 2: 28.
Pettigrew, Thomas (1985), "New Patterns of Racism: The Different Worlds of 1984 and 1964," *Rutgers Law Review*, Vol. 37: 673–706.
Polsby, Nelson (1963), *Community Power and Political Theory* (New Haven: Yale University Press).
President's Commission for the Study of Ethical Problems in Medicine and Biomedical and Behavioral Research (1983), *Making Health Care Decisions* (Washington, D.C.: U.S. Government Printing Office).
Rabin, Robert (1986), "Federal Regulation in Historical Perspective," *Stanford Law Review*, Vol. 38: 1189–1326.
Rawls, John (1971), *A Theory of Justice* (Cambridge: Harvard University Press).
Reich, Charles (1964), "The New Property," *Yale Law Journal*, Vol. 73: 733–787.

Rorty, Richard (1985), "Habermas and Lyotard on Postmodernity," in Richard Bernstein, ed., *Habermas and Modernity* (Cambridge: MIT Press): 160–175.
——— (1989), *Contingency, Irony, and Solidarity* (New York: Cambridge U. Press).
Rose-Ackerman, Susan (1988), "Progressive Law and Economics—and the New Administrative Law," *Yale Law Journal*, Vol. 98: 341–368.
Rosenberg, Maurice (1986), "Query: Can Court-Related Alternatives Improve Our Dispute Resolution System?" *Judicature*, Vol. 69: 254.
Sabatier, Paul, and Daniel Mazmanian (1981), "Relationships Between Governing Boards and Professional Staff: Role Orientations and Influence on the California Coastal Commission," *Administration & Society*, Vol. 13: 207–250.
Sandel, Michael (1982), *Liberalism and the Limits of Justice* (Cambridge: Cambridge University Press).
Scales, Anne (1986), "The Emergence of Feminist Jurisprudence: An Essay," *Yale Law Journal*, Vol. 95: 1375–1403.
Scholz, John (1984), "Cooperation, Deterrence, and the Ecology of Regulatory Enforcement," *Law and Society Review*, Vol. 18: 178–224.
Schulhofer, Stephen (1984), "Is Plea Bargaining Inevitable?" *Harvard Law Review*, Vol. 97: 1037–1107.
Shapiro, Martin (1983), "Administrative Discretion: The Next Stage," *Yale Law Journal*, Vol. 92: 1487–1522.
Shapiro, Sidney, and Thomas McGarity (1989), "Reorienting OSHA: Regulatory Alternatives and Legislative Reform," *Yale Journal on Regulation*, Vol. 6: 1–63.
Shapiro, Susan (1987), "The Social Control of Impersonal Trust," *American Journal of Sociology*, Vol. 93: 623–658.
Silbey, Susan (1980–81), "Case Processing: Consumer Protection in an Attorney General's Office," *Law & Society Review*, Vol. 15: 849–881.
Simon, William (1983), "Legality, Bureaucracy, and Class in the Welfare System," *Yale Law Journal*, Vol. 92: 1198–1269.
——— (1985), "The Invention and Reinvention of Welfare Rights," *Maryland Law Review*, Vol. 44: 1–37.
——— (1986), "Rights and Redistribution in the Welfare System," *Stanford Law Review*, Vol. 38: 1431–1516.
Skinner, Quentin, ed. (1985), *The Return of Grand Theory in the Humane Sciences* (Cambridge: Cambridge University Press).
Smith, Gilbert (1981), "Discretionary Decision-Making in Social Work," in Michael Adler and Stewart Asquith, eds., *Discretion and Welfare* (London: Heinemann Educational Books): 47–68.
Steiner, Peter (1983), "The Legalization of American Society: Economic Regulation," *Michigan Law Review*, Vol. 81: 1285–1306.
Stewart, Richard (1981), "Regulation, Innovation, and Administrative Law: A Conceptual Framework," *California Law Review*, Vol. 69: 1255–1377.

Stone, Alan (1979), "Informed Consent: Special Problems for Psychiatry," *Hospital & Community Psychiatry*, Vol. 30: 231–327.
Sunstein, Cass (1988), Book Review, "Feminism and Legal Theory," *Harvard Law Review*, Vol. 101: 826–848.
Teubner, Gunther (1983), "Substantive and Reflexive Elements in Modern Law," *Law and Society Review*, Vol. 17: 239–295.
——— (1984), "Autopoiesis in Law and Society: A Reply to Blankenburg," *Law and Society Review*, Vol. 18: 291–301.
——— (1986), "After Legal Instrumentalism? Strategic Models of Post-Regulatory Law," in Gunther Teubner, ed., *Dilemmas of Law in the Welfare State* (Berlin: Walter de Gruyter): 299–325.
——— (1988a), "Evolution of Autopoietic Law," in Gunther Teubner, ed., *Autopoietic Law: A New Approach to Law and Society* (Berlin: Walter de Gruyter): 217–241.
——— (1988b), "Introduction to Autopoietic Law," in Gunther Teubner, ed., *Autopoietic Law*, 1–11.
Tushnet, Mark (1986), "Critical Legal Studies: An Introduction to Its Origins and Underpinnings," *Journal of Legal Education*, Vol. 36: 505–517.
Unger, Roberto (1975), *Knowledge and Politics* (New York: The Free Press).
Vladeck, Bruce (1980), *Unloving Care: The Nursing Home Tragedy* (New York: Basic Books).
Weissert, William (1985), "Seven Reasons Why It Is so Difficult to Make Community-Based Care Cost-Effective," *HSR: Health Services Research*, Vol. 20: 423–433.
Wellmer, Albrecht (1985), "Reason, Utopia, and the *Dialectics of Enlightenment*," in Richard Bernstein, ed., *Habermas and Modernity* (Cambridge: MIT Press): 35–66.
West, Cornel (1988), "Law, Deconstruction, and the Resistance to Theory," *Journal of Law and Society*, Vol. 15: 166–187.
West, Robin (1988), "Jurisprudence and Gender," *University of Chicago Law Review*, Vol. 55: 1–72.
Wexler, Steven (1970), "Practicing Law for Poor People," *Yale Law Journal*, Vol. 79: 1049–1067.
Williams, Patricia J. (1987), "Alchemical Notes: Reconstructing Ideals from Deconstructed Rights," *Harvard Civil Rights–Civil Liberties Law Review*, Vol. 22: 401–433.
Winkler, J. T. (1986), "The Political Economy of Administrative Discretion," in Michael Adler and Stewart Asquith, eds., *Discretion and Welfare* (London: Heinemann Educational Books): 82–134.
Winter, Gerd (1985), "Bartering Rationality in Regulation," *Law and Society Review*, Vol. 19: 219–250.
Wolff, Robert (1968), *The Poverty of Liberalism* (Boston: Beacon Press).
Yngvesson, Barbara (1988), "Disputing Alternatives: Settlement as Science and as Politics," *Law and Social Inquiry*, Vol. 13: 113–132.
Young, Iris (1986), "The Ideal of Community and the Politics of Difference," *Social Theory and Practice*, Vol. 12: 1–26.

Zald, Mayer (1970), "Political Economy: A Framework for Comparative Analysis," in M. Zald, ed., *Power in Organizations* (Nashville: Vanderbilt University Press): 221–261.

Cases

City of Richmond v. J. A. Crosen Company (1989), 109 S.Ct. 706.

Index

Abel, Richard, 50
Accountability, 155–156
Ackerman, Bruce, 46, 47
Administrative Conference of the United States, 80
Aid to Families with Dependent Children, 32
Alternative dispute resolution, 50–54, 84
Altman, Andrew, 63
American Bar Association, 49
American College of Surgeons, 109
American Medical Association, 109
Antiprofessionalism, 49
Arbitration, 51
Arendt, Hannah, 85, 93, 132
Aristotle, 87
Autonomy, 3–5, 15–17, 19, 31; in alternative dispute resolution, 54; and communal interests, 5; and community, 66, 70, 96; in physician-patient relationship, 109; of social subsystems, 76
Autopoiesis, 77–78
Axelrod, Robert, 45, 46, 49, 131, 143

Bachrach, Peter, 22, 24
Baier, Annette, 99, 100, 101, 102, 103, 128, 129, 131, 133, 134, 138, 141, 161
Baker, C. Edwin, 104
Baratz, Morton, 22, 24
Bardach, Eugene, 41, 42, 49, 131
Bargaining, as dialogue, 49
Bernstein, Richard, 85, 86, 87, 88, 91, 92, 93, 94, 96, 97, 105, 138, 141
Blacks, legal rights of, 65–66
Blaming, 27

Boden, Deirdre, 23
Bureaucracy, 55, 60, 71
Bureaucratization, of social relationships, 74–75
Burger, Warren, 50
Bush, Robert, 54

Cartesian anxiety, 87
Christman, John, 16
Chronically ill patients, 111–113, 125
Citizen, and state relations, 107
Civil rights, 65–66
Claiming, 27
Clean Air Act, 46
Client and agency relationship, 75, 76, 125; divergence of interests, 59; inequality in, 156
Client empowerment strategies, 123
Clients: attributes of, 59; moral qualities of, 58; status as a function of values, 30; as subject or object, 31
Coates, Dan, 27
Collective bargaining, 79
Colonization of the life-world, 34, 74
Communication, 92–93
Communicative: action, 90–91; advocacy, 159; conflict, 116; reason, 92
Communities, participatory, 10
Community, 54, 70, 98–106, 127–134, 137–142; -based care for frail, elderly poor, 8, 118–127; conditions of, 143–161; constitutive, 94–95; creation of, 138–139; elitism in, 141; empowerment, 51; and individualism, 95–96; instrumental, 84; literature, 5; partial, autonomy in, 140; partial creation of, 138,

140–141; participation in, 98; sentimental, 94
Connection thesis, 68
Connolly, William, 16, 17
Continental theorists. *See* Reflexive law
Continuing relationships, 20
Cooperation, 46, 107; instrumental, 98, 132; sentimental, 98
Co-optation, 11, 57, 160–161
Cornell, Drucilla, 91, 96
Crenshaw, Kimberlé, 66
Critical legal theory, 7, 60, 62–66, 68, 69, 72; as a male theory, 68
Culture of silence, 25, 135

Decentering, 64
Decentralization, 10, 153–158
Decisionism, 86
Deconstruction, 65
Demystification, 63
Dependent people, 6, 13–38; and bureaucracies, 1; as equals, 131; and the welfare state, 4, 7
Deregulation, 49, 80–81
Dewey, John, 105
Dialogical community, 5, 94–99, 156, 161
Dialogism, 85–106, 107, 128, 139, 145, 147; in bureaucracy, 157; in community-based care for frail, elderly poor, 144; conditions of, 143–148; in informed consent, 144; purposive, 131; in special education, 144
Dialogue, 97, 153; threat of, to experts, 89
Discretion, 6, 15, 17–21, 31–32, 40, 45, 58, 61, 84, 144, 153, 154; control of, 83; and dependent people, 4; informal, 40; in regulation, 60; in welfare state, 3
Disputing, 25–28, 54
Downward professionalism, 144, 148, 155

Eagleton, Terry, 141
Economic efficiency, 48
Edelman, Murray, 24, 33, 34
Education for All Handicapped Children Act, 114–118
Elmore, Richard, 154
Empowerment, 98, 134–137, 148–152, 158–161; and autonomy of dependent people, 5; of chronically ill, 132; of dependent people, 136; of frail, elderly poor, 133; commitment to, by for-profit community care agencies, 124; in special education, 133
Enforcement, field, 43–44

England. *See* Water pollution control
English, Terry, 97
Enlightenment, 92
Entitlements, 2, 6, 33
Environment of organizations, 56–57
Environmental Protection Agency, 47

Feminism: and bureaucracy, 70–72; liberal legal, 67
Feminist jurisprudence, 7, 62, 66–72
Feminists: communitarian, 67–72, 80–85, 95, 139; cultural, 68–69; radical, 69
Ferguson, Kathy, 70, 71, 72, 139, 140, 147
Formal equality, 65
Formal rationalization, 83
Formalism, 6, 50
Frail, elderly poor. *See* Community-based care for frail, elderly poor
Freire, Paulo, 25
Friedman, Marilyn, 95
Functional independence, 124

Gabel, Peter, 65
Gadamer, Hans-Georg, 85, 88, 89, 93, 96, 97
Game theory, 45–46
Garbage can model, 56, 60
Gaventa, John, 25, 33, 61
Goodwill, 99, 133
Gramsci, Antonio, 24, 33, 34

Habermas, Jürgen, 34, 48, 61, 72, 73, 74, 75, 76, 78, 79, 82, 85, 90, 91, 92, 93, 96, 99, 104, 139, 140
Handicapped children. *See* Special education
Harrington, Christine, 80, 81
Hasenfeld, Yeheskel, 28, 29, 30, 31, 55, 57, 58, 59, 61, 99, 143, 144, 149, 150, 151, 152, 153, 155, 156, 158
Hawkins, Keith, 43, 44, 46, 49, 53, 61, 99, 131, 143
Health care. *See* Chronically ill patients; Informed consent; Physician-patient
Held, Virginia, 101
Hermeneutics, 88, 89, 97–98
Human service agencies, 28–34, 55–59

Ideal speech, 79, 90–92, 139–140
Ideology, 17; of social workers, 143–144
Implementation analysis, 60–61
Impression management, 71
Individualism, 15–17, 70, 85

Informal: caregivers, 118–127; discretion, 20–21; justice, 49–54
Informed consent, 8, 35, 38, 107–113, 117
Injustice, tolerance for, 26
Innovation, 44
Institute of Medicine, 126–127
Institutions, meaning of, 64
Interdependence, 4
Intimacy, 68–69

Juridification, 74–76
Jurisprudence, theories of, 62–82

Kagan, Robert, 41, 42, 49, 131
Kantian: liberalism, 94–95, 105; rights, 84
Katz, Jay, 108, 110
Kuhn, Thomas, 87, 88

Law: as constitution, 81, 153; ideology in, 64; indeterminacy of, 62; as institution, 74, 76; as male domination, 67; as medium, 74; neutrality of, 62–63; normative values in, 73; policy analysis in, 63; political values in, 63; substantive rationality in, 76
Legal: -bureaucratic regime, 107, 144; realism, 62–64; rights, 53–55, 65–67, 145, 157; rights revolution, 2–6, 41; system, contextualization of, 72; system, illegitimacy of, 64; system, reflexivity in, 78
Legitimation crisis, 2
Liberal legalism, 3, 6; attack on, 62, 85; failure of, 2, 34; flaws in, 19–21; focus of, 84–86; as a male theory of, 68–70; view of rights, 14
Liberal society, 92–93
Lidz, Charles, 111
Litigation crisis, 49–50
Luhmann, Niklas, 48, 60, 61, 73, 76, 77, 78, 99
Lukes, Steven, 22, 61

MacIntyre, Alasdair, 96, 97
MacKinnon, Catharine, 69
Madison, Wisconsin. *See* Special education
March, James, 56, 60
Masculine jurisprudence. *See* Critical legal theory
Medicaid, 119, 121
Medical malpractice. *See* Informed consent
Medicare, 122–124
Meisel, Alan, 111
Menkel-Meadow, Carrie, 51, 53, 54, 61

Modern/postmodern communitarian ethics, 85–106
Molotch, Harvey, 23
Moral typification, 30–31, 61
Morality, 68–69; of associations, 103–104

Naming, 27–28
Natural systems, 55
Negotiated rule-making, 43–45
Negotiation, 51–54, 80–82
Normative values, 61
Nursing homes, 118–120, 125–127

Objectivism, 86–87
Occupational Safety and Health Administration, 40–43, 47–48
Open systems, 55–56
Organizations, 55–61

Participatory exceptions, 107–127
Paternalism of physicians, 108–111
Patriarchy, 67–71
Penrod, Steven, 27
Phronesis, 87–89, 97–99
Physician-patient: dialogue, 108–113; relationship, 34–38
Political economy theory, 28–31, 56–59
Pollution: auctioning of permits, 46–48. *See also* Water pollution control
Poor, deserving and undeserving, 33
Power: in alternative dispute resolution, 54; in communication, 98; control of, 84–85; and dependency in client-staff relationships, 59; dimensions of, 21–25; in feminist jurisprudence, 66, 70; in human service agencies, 28–34, 57; manifestations of, 134; as a normative concern, 61; organizational, 59; in social service relationships, 7, 135; and social work practice theory, 148–152
Practical philosophy, 88–90
Practice ideologies, 30–31
Praxis. *See* Practical philosophy
Presidential Commission for the Study of Ethical Problems in Medicine and Biomedical and Behavioral Research, 108
Procedural due process, 2–6
Professional norms, 29–31, 143–148, 151–152
Progressives, 63
Property rights, 13–15
Psychology of disputing, 25–28
Public space, 93–94

Quiescence, 21–28

Rationality: formal, 73; procedural, 91; purposive, 92; substantive, 73, 76–77, 91; system, 91; Weberian, 55, 60
Rawls, John, 94, 97, 98, 103, 104, 105
Reciprocal concrete incentives, 9, 10, 113, 139, 140; in community-based care for frail, elderly poor, 121, 122, 125, 130; and professional norms, 152, 157; in special education, 117–118; and trust, 127–129
Reconstructive jurisprudence, 69
Reflexive law, 7–8, 48, 62, 72–82, 84, 140, 154; regulation through, 78–79
Regulation, 39–49; bargaining in, 45; command-and-control, 4, 7, 40, 43, 46, 48, 61, 80; compliance, 44–45; conciliatory, 40, 43; cooperative-style, 7, 44, 61, 80, 82; crisis of, 39, 40, 73, 77; effect on social systems, 48; and individuality, 49; of informal care, 122; legal-bureaucratic, 8; legalistic, 42; participation in, 80; participatory, 8, 9; reciprocity in, 44
Regulatory: failure, 117; goals, 45–49; negotiation, 80–81; reform, 46–49, 55; role of state, 1–2, 80–81; unreasonableness, 39–49
Reich, Charles, 13
Reimbursement formulae, 155
Relativism, 86–87
Renal dialysis. See Chronically ill patients
Rorty, Richard, 85, 92, 93, 105
Rose-Ackerman, Susan, 47

Sandel, Michael, 84, 94, 95, 96, 104, 105, 138
Science, 87–88
Self: conceptions of, 105; -determination, 31–38, 148–152; regulation, 77–79
Separation thesis, 68–69
Shared decision-making, 34–38; in community-based care for frail, elderly poor, 118–125; in medicine, 108–113; in special education, 116–118
Simon, Herbert, 55
Simon, William, 144, 145, 147, 148, 149, 152, 155, 157, 158
Social: engineering, 78; movement groups, 158–161; planning, 77; service agencies as moral systems, 135; subsystems, 76–81, 140; values, 63; work contract, 149; work practice theory, 28–31, 145–152

Socialization of elites, 64–65
Sociology of organizations, 4–6, 55–61
Socratic: discourse, 91; virtues, 93
Solidarity, 66
Special education, 8, 114–118, 125, 159–160. See also Dialogism; Empowerment
Speech acts, 90–92
State-market relations, 80–81
Stewart, Richard, 44, 46, 47
Structured coupling, 60
System theory, 76–77

Taylorism, 55
Technology, 30–31, 56–58. See also Human service agencies
Teubner, Gunther, 60, 61, 73, 77, 78, 79
Therapeutic state, 51, 75
Trade-off programs, 47
Trust, 128–132; between client and worker, 31; in community-based care for frail, elderly poor, 125; in the dialogical community, 99–103; morally decent, 136, 140; in treatment of chronically ill patients, 113
Tushnet, Mark, 63

Urban relationships, 95
Utilitarianism, 84–85
Utility maximization, 46

Values, 84
Violent abstraction, 74
Vladeck, Bruce, 127

War on Poverty, 11, 161
Water pollution control, 8, 43–46, 99, 131
Weber, Max, 73, 83
Weberian: bureaucracy, 153; efficiency, 144; ideology, 156
Welfare state, 13–14, 61, 81; modern, criticism of, 2, 72–77; and dependent people, 6; and the individual, 3
West, Robin, 68, 69
Williams, Patricia J., 65, 66
Women, 67. See also Feminism; Feminists
Work and welfare, 33

Yngvesson, Barbara, 54, 61

Zald, Mayer, 56
Zero-sum, 46, 52–53
Zone: of freedom, 15–17, 31–34; of privacy, 14

University of Pennsylvania Press
Law in Social Context Series
Keith Hawkins and John M. Thomas, Series Editors

Richard Lempert and Joseph Sanders. *An Invitation to Law and Social Science.* 1986.
Joseph Rees. *Reforming the Workplace: A Study in Self-Regulation in Occupational Safety.* 1988.
Jeffrey A. Roth, John T. Scholz, and Ann Dryden Witte, eds. *Taxpayer Compliance Volume I: An Agenda for Research.* 1989.
Jeffrey A. Roth and John T. Scholz, eds. *Taxpayer Compliance Volume II: Social Science Perspectives.* 1989.
Joel F. Handler. *Law and the Search for Community.* 1990.

LIBRARY OF DAVIDSON

Books on regular loan may be ch